Reforming Juvenile Detention

No More Hidden Closets

Edited by

Ira M. Schwartz
and William H. Barton

Ohio State University Press / Columbus

Library of Congress Cataloging-in-Publication Data

Reforming juvenile detention : no more hidden closets / edited by Ira
M. Schwartz and William H. Barton.
p. cm.
Includes bibliographical references (p.   ) and index.
ISBN 0–8142–0635–2 (cloth : acid-free paper). — ISBN
0–8142–0636–0 (pbk. : acid-free paper)
1. Juvenile detention—United States. 2. Juvenile corrections—
United States. 3. Juvenile justice, Administration of—United
States. I. Schwartz, Ira M. II. Barton, William H., 1949– .
HV9104.R42 1994
364'.42'0973—dc20   94–11832
CIP

Text design by Nighthawk Design.
Type set in Palatino by Connell-Zeko, Kansas City, Mo.
Printed by Bookcrafters, Chelsea, Mi.

The paper in this book meets the guidelines for permanence and durability of
the Committee on Production Guidelines for Book Longevity of the Council on
Library Resources.
∞

9 8 7 6 5 4 3 2

To Andrew, David, and Amy

Contents

Introduction

Juvenile Detention: No More Hidden Closets

WILLIAM H. BARTON
AND IRA M. SCHWARTZ

On any given day, more than 18,000 young people can be found in the nation's public juvenile detention centers (Krisberg & Herrera, 1991). They sleep in tiny, barren cells, often wear "institutional green" uniforms, march single file to and from classes and meals, and sometimes remain locked up for several weeks, and even months, only to be sent home after they finally have their day in court.

Juvenile detention was termed the "hidden closet for the skeletons of the rest of the system" by Patricia Wald in 1975 (see Schwartz et al., 1987). In 1987, Schwartz et al. analyzed national statistics on the rate of detention use in the country and subtitled their article "The Hidden Closets Revisited." At that time, it appeared that secure juvenile detention was being used increasingly—and often inappropriately—in many jurisdictions. A look at yet more recent data is hardly reassuring—even more facilities are overcrowded and continue to hold many relatively low-risk youths at great and unnecessary expense. Although other areas of the juvenile justice system have received close scrutiny and show some signs of improvement, detention issues appear to have been relegated to low priority. Fiscal concerns alone will not permit states and counties to continue to ignore detention.

Detention centers are essentially jails for juveniles who have been arrested and are awaiting trial and are intended to hold those thought to be the most dangerous or the most likely to abscond prior to their court hearings. Since the juvenile justice reforms of the 1970s, we as a nation no longer hold large numbers of juveniles in adult jails. Juvenile detention centers would thus seem to be an improvement. But are they?

A closer look shows that many detention facilities are not only overcrowded and in poor physical condition but also hold many youths who do not seem to need such costly, secure confinement. *Some* detained youths have prior records and alleged offenses, which suggests that they are highly dangerous and/or likely to flee, but just as many youths—or more—do not appear to pose much of a risk to public safety. This latter group ends up in detention because communities and various children's service agencies have failed to find more positive alternatives for them.

When families, neighborhoods, schools, and other programs no longer wish to deal with troubled children, the detention center is the one resource that cannot turn them away. This is an unacceptable excuse for imposing such a costly and potentially damaging experience upon these children. The time has come to confront current juvenile detention practices throughout the country and to develop policies and practices that reserve secure detention for the truly dangerous juvenile offender, while finding other ways to deal with the rest of the youths who currently languish "behind the closet door" in detention facilities.

This book pulls together data on national trends in detention policies and practices, along with practical summaries of reform targets and strategies. The authors represent a mix of policy, research, and practice perspectives. The current trends in detention are disturbing, and this book includes concrete suggestions for improvements. The basic approach is simple: reserve detention for those who pose a truly high risk to public safety; develop ways to accurately assess the degree of risk an individual juvenile presents; develop less costly and less restrictive alternatives for the lower-risk youths; and closely monitor and evaluate the new detention practices and policies. These methods have been applied in some jurisdictions with promising results, as will be shown in succeeding chapters. This book both presents a picture of a more rational structuring of detention and provides a discussion of political strategies that may help bring about the necessary policy changes.

Juvenile Detention as a Policy Issue

Juvenile detention is an issue that has received less attention than have training schools, diversion, and other aspects of the juvenile justice system (Schwartz et al., 1987). Its purpose, according to most states' statutes, is limited to the secure, pretrial confinement of youths who pose an unacceptably high risk of failing to appear for court hearings or of committing offenses in the interim period. It is not intended to be used as a post-adjudicatory commitment placement, for punishment, for administrative convenience, or because of a lack of detention alternatives. Furthermore, detained youths are supposed to be given detention hearings, usually within one or two days, at which time the court is expected to review the grounds for detention. Thus, the purpose and process of juvenile detention—to be limited to high risk cases, and designed to protect both public safety and the child's rights—appear clear.

Yet national statistics, as discussed in more detail by Schwartz and Willis in chapter 1, consistently reveal extensive overcrowding and misuse of secure detention, along with staggering geographical disparities in the rate of detention use. These trends have been apparent for some time (e.g., Krisberg & Herrera, 1991; Krisberg & Schwartz, 1983; Schwartz et al., 1987; Steketee et al., 1989) and appear to have worsened in recent years.

There are several reasons why policymakers should view the growing problems of juvenile detention with alarm. First, secure detention is a very costly use of scarce juvenile justice resources. Per diem operating costs range from $70 to $150 per bed. National operating expenditures for juvenile detention have more than doubled in the last decade, reaching a total of $513 million in 1989 (Krisberg & Herrera, 1991). Construction costs for new detention facilities are estimated at between $75,000 and $100,000 per bed. Thus detention, intended to be neither punishment nor treatment, can consume large portions of a state's juvenile justice budget. For example, Florida in 1988 allocated fully 40% of its delinquency programs budget to the operation of detention (Orlando & Barton, 1989).

Second, detention can have harmful effects on the detained youths. Several specific incidences of abuse and/or wretched conditions have prompted lawsuits (see Dale, forthcoming, for a review and analysis of litigation related to juvenile detention). In addition to such specific harms, several studies have demonstrated that youths who have been securely detained are more likely to receive subsequent out-of-home placements in either juvenile justice, child welfare, or mental health settings, even when the analyses controlled for other relevant factors, including offense and prior history (Feld, 1988; Fitzharris, 1985; Frazier

& Bishop, 1985; Krisberg & Schwartz, 1983; McCarthy, 1987). It would appear that judges and others who make placement decisions sometimes view a youth's detention itself as evidence of the need for continuing out-of-home placement.

Third, detention appears to be used increasingly for youths *after* adjudication who are awaiting placement in commitment programs. According to recent national statistics, the admission of committed youths to public detention centers has increased five-fold from 1977 to 1987 (Steketee et al., 1989). These youths often stay in detention longer, thus placing additional strains on available bedspace. Moreover, the commingling of pre-adjudication and post-adjudication youths raises serious questions of appropriateness.

It is time for juvenile justice policymakers to confront juvenile detention issues head on. Does it make sense to devote such a large share of resources to a part of the system that is not intended or designed to have any impact beyond holding allegedly dangerous youths prior to their adjudicatory hearings? Are there not less costly alternatives that could be more widely used for many of the youths currently being detained? Who decides which youths will be securely detained, and upon what criteria are such decisions based? How long do youths spend in these facilities, and can the lengths of stay be reduced? What kinds of programming should, and should not, be implemented in detention centers? What kinds of due process protections should be available to youths at the point of detention admissions decisions and during any stays in detention? The answers to such questions will profoundly affect the future of juvenile justice systems in this country.

An Agenda for Detention Reform

How can one bring about improvements in juvenile detention policies and practices? First, one must recognize that detention capacity is less related to such determinate factors as the size of a jurisdiction's youth population or juvenile crime rates than one might think. In chapter 2, Martin presents a historical analysis of the detention practices in Cuyahoga County, Ohio, clearly demonstrating that the number of youths held in secure detention is primarily a function of policy decisions which are independent of demographic and crime statistics. As another example, Florida adopted sweeping legislative reform of juvenile detention practices in 1980. These reforms succeeded in reducing secure detention usage by about 20% and were not accompanied by increased threats to public safety (Florida Department of HRS 1981; McNeese & Ezell, 1983). But despite these successes, the Florida legislature overturned the reforms the following year, and detention rates rose immediately. During none of the years in question were there marked changes in the size of Florida's youth population or the rate of juvenile arrests. Such studies show that juvenile justice policymakers possess the ability to affect the rate of detention usage by implementing and monitoring specific policy objectives.

Targets for Change

Attempts to reduce the use of secure juvenile detention should focus on three primary areas: development of objective intake criteria and procedures that consistently limit admissions to secure detention; creation of less restrictive alternatives for some youths who do not require secure detention but who do require some level of supervision; and case-monitoring procedures that insure that youths are moved out of detention as quickly as possible. Of course, the attention given to reducing the use of secure detention does not obviate the need for providing adequate conditions of confinement for those who must still be securely detained. The next sections outline these issues.

Intake Criteria

Recent attempts to implement objective intake criteria have met with considerable success. In California, several jurisdictions have adopted objective guidelines developed by the National Council on Crime and Delinquency, as discussed by Steinhart in chapter 3. A similar approach was part of the Center for the Study of Youth Policy's Broward County Detention Project in Florida as described in chapter 4. Evaluations of these and similar programs have shown that objective intake criteria can reduce admissions to secure detention and do not jeopardize public safety. Typically, rearrest rates for youths released while on detention status and rates of failure to appear for court hearings are between 5 and 15% (Community Research Center, 1983; Kihm, 1980; Schwartz, Barton, & Orlando, 1991; Steinhart, 1990).

Detention Alternatives

Some jurisdictions have developed viable home detention programs that have helped limit the use of secure detention. The first juvenile home detention program was started in St. Louis in the early 1970s (Keve & Zantec, 1972). Other notable programs were developed in Jefferson County (Louisville), Kentucky (Community Research Center, 1983) and Cuyahoga County (Cleveland), Ohio (Ball, Huff, & Lilly, 1988). In such programs, workers are assigned small caseloads—ten or fewer—and expected to have one or more daily contacts with the youths at irregular times, to be on call 24 hours a day for crisis intervention, and to have frequent contacts with parents, schools, and other agencies as needed. All of these programs have demonstrated admirable success rates: 5 to 10% failing to appear at hearings and 10 to 20% acquiring additional charges.

Non-secure residential programs—e.g., shelters, family crisis homes, and proctor homes—and daytime report centers can effectively supplement home detention. Some youths are securely detained not because of dangerous offense profiles but because they lack viable homes. Others may be detained because they are neither working nor in school, and this lack of structure is perceived by many judges and other decision makers as making them an unacceptable risk. The Broward County Detention Project (chapter 4) mentioned above also included the development of a shelter program and a daytime report center run by private agencies. These programs greatly enhanced the effectiveness and credibility of the home detention program.

Length of Stay

The size of the detention population at any time is a function of two variables: admissions and length of stay. The design and development of both intake criteria and detention alternatives are intended to reduce the rate of admissions to secure detention. Strategies for reducing length of stay, however, are less clear cut. Prompt judicial review is essential, and most jurisdictions require detention hearings within one or two days of admission. Similarly, many states place limits on time-to-trial, but these limits are often exceeded as a result of case continuances requested by either prosecutors or defense attorneys. In the late 1980s, Cuyahoga County, Ohio, implemented highly aggressive case-monitoring practices that expedited court processing and reduced detention stays which resulted in sharp decreases in the average daily population in secure detention (as described by Sanniti in chapter 5). These practices included the use of a sophisticated information system that permitted instant tracking of a youth's detention status and court schedule, immediate access to court docketing, a system of around-the-clock detention hearings conducted by special referees, and the assignment of responsibility for case tracking to an official with sufficient authority within the court system to see that policies were carried out.

Conditions of Confinement

Of course, secure detention will always be needed for some youths. With the kinds of alternatives and procedures described above, however, the number of such youths should be more manageable than is currently the case in most jurisdictions. An example of a well-run secure detention program is described by Christy in chapter 6.

Strategies for Change

One must recognize that existing detention policies and practices have evolved from working relationships among several agencies and key actors, each pursuing a variety of interests, not all of which are compatible. The use of secure detention is in line with the interests of judges, prosecutors, and law enforcement officials, who must answer to the public for any threats to public safety. Their tolerance for risks posed by youths on pre-trial status is understandably lower than that of detention administrators, child advocates, and defense attorneys, for whom overcrowding and overuse of detention are seen as highly problematic. The general public's interests are mixed—they demand protection from crime but also must foot the bill for costly protection.

The implementation of policy changes requires a merging of ideas and incentives: development of both the political "will" to initiate the changes and the technical "way" to carry them out. The ideas, the technical "ways," are there—objective intake criteria, a range of alternative programs, diligent case monitoring, etc. Developing the political will is the greater challenge. Political will can be influenced by consensus strategies, by conflict strategies, or by some combination of both. Consensus strategies may have a better potential for bringing about lasting change but sometimes prove insufficient in overcoming strong initial resistance. Both consensus and conflict strategies have been used in detention reform efforts, and both have their advantages and limitations.

Consensus Strategies

As outlined by Barton in chapter 8, the best potential opportunity for consensus lies in promoting the goal of cost effectiveness. A cost-effective detention policy would place strict limits on the use of expensive secure detention. Non-secure alternatives for many youths currently being detained would provide adequate public safety protection at far less cost. The resulting savings could be applied to other juvenile justice and child welfare programs. A related incentive is the avoidance of some long-term costs associated with subsequent out-of-home placements. Additional incentives can be provided by the possibility of external funding for the development of alternative detention programs, as was the case with the Casey Foundation's funding of the Broward County Project. There may be additional fiscal incentives from the potential access to federal funding streams for detention alternatives (Center for the Study of Social Policy, 1990).

Beyond a consideration of incentives, there are several keys to the process of managing policy change in this or any other area. First, legislation can play a major role in guiding policy development and implementation. Second, the use of local task forces made up of relevant key decision makers (at a minimum, representatives of the judiciary, prosecutors, public defenders, executive juvenile justice agencies, and youth advocates) may enhance the potential for sustained reforms. Third, a key implementing official must be identified, someone who has sufficient authority within the jurisdiction, who is viewed as credible by all relevant parties and is able to maintain a high level of commitment to the reform policies throughout the many months, and even years, that such change efforts require. Finally, careful evaluations of change efforts are necessary to ensure that policy objectives are met.

Litigation

When consensus strategies are insufficient to overcome resistance to change, or fail as a means to bring the relevant parties to the table in the first place, the threat or actual filing of class-action lawsuits against overcrowded detention facilities can serve as a negative reinforcement to motivate change. Lawsuits have played a major role in several change efforts, including the San Francisco and Broward County projects discussed in chapters 3 and 4. In chapter 7, Anderson and Schwartz describe the use of litigation to bring about statewide detention reform in Pennsylvania. Different jurisdictions may require different mixes of incentives.

The Role of the Judiciary

Failure to obtain judicial support can severely, and perhaps fatally, limit the effectiveness of detention reform efforts. Judges in general often resist the introduction of objective intake guidelines and other mechanisms embodied in many detention reform efforts. In particular, judges often use the "valid court order exception" to order the detention of status offenders or others who might be excluded from detention according to various other criteria. These issues are explored by Judge McCully, who argues in chapter 9 that judges need not be fearful of detention reform efforts.

Toward a National Reform Agenda

In the final chapter, Schwartz summarizes the preceding sections and offers a clarion call for a national reform agenda in juvenile detention. Fiscal realities will no longer permit policymakers to ignore juvenile detention. Detention has become a dumping ground to compensate for other inadequacies within both our communities and our youth-serving programs. As a short-term holding facility, it does relatively little to protect long-term public safety, while it unnecessarily increases the likelihood that many youths will continue to require costly out-of-home care far into the future. The time has come to confront these realities and move forward. Only by focusing on detention issues, developing alternatives, and facilitating changes such as those described in this book can policymakers truly bring juvenile detention "out of the closet" and into its proper, albeit limited place within a more rational juvenile justice system.

Bibliography

Ball, R. A., Huff, C. R., & Lilly, J. R. (1988). *House arrest and correctional policy: Doing time at home.* Newbury Park, CA: Sage.

Center for the Study of Social Policy. (1990). *Refinancing Broward County's juvenile justice system.* Washington, D.C.: Center for the Study of Social Policy.

Community Research Center. (1983). *A community response to a crisis: The effective use of detention and alternatives to detention in Jefferson County, Kentucky.* Washington, D.C.: U.S. Department of Juvenile Justice and Delinquency Prevention.

Dale, M. J. (forthcoming). The role of litigation in correcting conditions in juvenile detention centers.

Feld, B. C. (1988). *In re Gault* revisited: A cross-state comparison of the right to counsel in juvenile court. *Crime and Delinquency, 34,* 393–424.

Fitzharris, T. L. (1985). *The foster children in California: Profiles of 10,000 children in residential care.* Sacramento, CA: Children's Services Foundation.

Florida Department of Health and Rehabilitative Services. (1981). *A report on the impact of detention-related changes made in the Juvenile Justice Act in 1980.* Tallahassee: HRS, Office of Evaluation and Children, Youth and Families Program Office.

Frazier, C., & Bishop, D. (1985). The pretrial detention of juveniles and its impact on case dispositions. *Journal of Criminal Law and Criminology, 76,* 1132–52.

Keve, P. W., & Zantek, C. S. (1972). *Final report and evaluation of the home detention program, St. Louis, Missouri, September 30, 1971, to July 2, 1972.* McLean, VA: Research Analysis Corporation.

Kihm, R. C. (1980). *Prohibiting secure juvenile detention: Assessing the effectiveness of national standards detention criteria.* Champaign, IL: University of Illinois Community Research Forum.

Krisberg, B., & Herrera, N. C. (1991). *National juvenile detention statistical trends.* San Francisco: National Council on Crime and Delinquency.

Krisberg, B., & Schwartz, I. M. (1983). Rethinking juvenile justice. *Crime and Delinquency, 29,* 333–64.

McCarthy, B. R. (1987). Preventive detention and pretrial custody in the juvenile court. *Journal of Criminal Justice, 15,* 185–200.

McNeese, C. A., & Ezell, M. (1983). Political symbolism in juvenile justice:

Reforming Florida's juvenile detention criteria. *Journal of Sociology and Social Welfare, 10*, 242–58.

Orlando, F. A., & Barton, W. H. (1989). *The juvenile detention crisis in Florida.* Ann Arbor, MI: Center for the Study of Youth Policy.

Schwartz, I. M., Barton, W. H., & Orlando, F. A. (1991). Keeping kids out of secure detention: The misuse of juvenile detention has a profound impact on child welfare. *Public Welfare, 49*(2), 20–26, 46.

Schwartz, I. M., Fishman, G., Hatfield, R. R., Krisberg, B., & Eisikovits, Z. (1987). Juvenile detention: The hidden closets revisited. *Justice Quarterly, 4,* 219–35.

Steinhart, D. (1990). *Testing the public safety impact of juvenile detention criteria applied at San Francisco's Youth Guidance Center.* San Francisco: National Council on Crime and Delinquency.

Steketee, M. W., Willis, D. A., & Schwartz, I. M. (1989). *Juvenile justice trends: 1977–1987.* Ann Arbor, MI: University of Michigan, Center for the Study of Youth Policy.

1

National Trends in Juvenile Detention

IRA M. SCHWARTZ
AND DEBORAH A. WILLIS

There are 422 public juvenile detention centers in the United States, more than twice the number of training schools. There are approximately 500,000 annual admissions to detention centers every year, more than nine times the number of admissions to training schools (Schwartz, Willis, & Battle, 1991). As outlined in the introduction, despite the enormous role detention centers play in the juvenile justice system, relatively little is known about these facilities. They are the "hidden closets" of the system (Schwartz, Fishman, Hatfield, Krisberg, & Eisikovits, 1987).

The purpose of this chapter is to explore the trends and issues which currently surround juvenile detention. We hope it will lead to a better understanding of the role of detention and more interest in detention-related issues on the part of academics, juvenile justice professionals, policymakers, and child advocates.

The Children in Custody biennial census was analyzed to examine the trends in detention over time. Begun in 1971 and administered by the United States Census Bureau, the census is a survey of public and private juvenile detention and correctional facilities designed to collect information about the facilities themselves and the youths who are placed in them. The survey has an extremely high response rate, never having fallen below a 96% return rate. Information used in this chapter concerns public facilities and was derived from analyses conducted by the Center for the Study of Youth Policy at the University of Michigan using census data from 1977 through 1988–89.

As comprehensive as this data set is, it has a number of significant limitations. Annual admissions data may include multiple counts of individual youths. The one-day counts are unduplicated, but probably give a somewhat skewed picture of the population because the more serious offenders have longer lengths of stay and thus have a higher probability of being confined in a juvenile facility on any given day. The accuracy of the information collected also depends on the varying ability and diligence of the individual employees filling out the forms. Finally, the data examined in this chapter only include juveniles held in public detention centers. It does not include juveniles held in adult jails.

National Detention Trends

Table 1.1 includes the numbers and rates of admissions to detention centers between 1971 and 1989. As can be seen, rates declined between 1974 and 1983, began to increase in 1985, and reached an all-time high in 1989. The rate of admission for males was relatively stable until 1987, when it began to increase sharply. The rate for females declined between 1974 and 1983 and has been on the rise ever since (Schwartz et al., 1991; Poulin, Levitt, Young, & Pappenfort, 1980).

State Detention Trends

The numbers and rates of youth incarcerated in detention centers vary tremendously among states (see table 1.2). In examining detention rates across the country during the 1970s, Poulin et al. found rates varying from a high of 4,734 per 100,000 eligible youth in California to a low of 44.7 per 100,000 in North Dakota (1980, 9). During 1988, 31 states had admissions rates ranging between 1,000 and 6,500 youth per 100,000, and 14 states had admissions rates under 1,000 youth per 100,000. Washington, D.C., stood alone ahead of everyone with a rate of 15,223 admissions for every 100,000 youth in the district (Schwartz, Steketee, & Willis, 1989).

Why have there been such wide variations in admission rates among states? Logic might indicate a connection between the amount of serious crime in a state and the number of youths detained. Amazingly, the factor explaining the greatest proportion of the variance among states is the number of public detention beds available (Krisberg, Litsky,

& Schwartz, 1984, 227; Poulin et al., 1980). Krisberg and his colleagues found the "number of detention beds per 100,000 (eligible) youth population explains 76.8 percent of the variation in detention rates" (Krisberg et al., 1984, 159–62). A similar procedure applied to the 1988 Census data using a stepwise multiple regression analysis found that bed rates (number of beds per 100,000 youth) combined with arrest rates for Part I and II offenses were significant ($p < .001$) in explaining 91% of the variance among states. However, Part I and II arrest rates added only 4.6% to the 86% explained by bed rates alone.

Poulin and his colleagues also found that "about 56% of all admissions to detention centers occurred in five states—California, Ohio, Texas, Washington, and Florida" (Poulin et al., 1980, 47). These same five states accounted for 52% of all admissions during fiscal year 1989 while they accounted for approximately 29% of the total eligible youth population (CIC, 1988).

Changes in Detention Practices

The national admissions data mask the fact that detention centers are undergoing a number of major changes. Post-adjudication usage is increasing, facilities are becoming more overcrowded, ethnic minority populations now make up the majority of admissions, and detention for status offenses has decreased while detention for violations of valid court orders has increased. These changes appear to have started in the late 1970s.

Commitment to Detention Centers

Although conceived and designed as pre-adjudication holding facilities, detention centers are increasingly being used for post-adjudication purposes. Confining pre- and post-adjudication populations in the same facility suggests that detention centers are playing the same role in the juvenile justice system that jails play in the adult criminal justice process (Schwartz et al., 1986).

Table 1.2 shows the rate of pre- and post-adjudication admissions to detention centers for all states. Twenty-nine of the 47 states that reported having a detention center indicated that such facilities were also used for committed youth. The extent of this practice varies greatly among these 29 states. For example, Washington State has the highest rate of committed youth in detention (1,156 per 100,000); West Virginia has the lowest rate (4 youth per 100,000) (Schwartz et al., 1991). The average rate of commitment admissions among states that use detention for this purpose is 143 youth per 100,000.

Overcrowded Conditions

The number of juveniles incarcerated in detention centers on any given day has skyrocketed. This has contributed to an increase in the number of facilities reporting overcrowded conditions. As reflected in table 1.3, there has been a steady increase in the number of over-crowded facilities and the proportion of incarcerated youth housed in such institutions. In 1979, 6.4% of public detention centers in the United States were over capacity, housing 8.8% of all youth incarcerated in detention centers. By 1989, 27.5% of the facilities were over capacity, housing 50.4% of all incarcerated youth (Schwartz et al., 1991). In fact, the proportion of youth confined in overcrowded facilities increased more than five-fold between 1979 and 1989 (Schwartz et al., 1991).

Detention centers are administered by the juvenile courts or by an agency in the executive branch of government. Approximately 45% of all public detention centers are administered by the courts, and 55% are administered by some other type of governmental agency at the state, county, or municipal level. Of the 188 facilities administered by the courts, 31 (16%) were reported to be overcrowded on the day the detention census was taken in 1989. In contrast, 85 of the 234 facilities (36%) administered by other agencies were reported to be overcrowded on that same day. Using a standard t-test, we found this to be significant at the $p < .01$ level, indicating that court-administered detention centers are less likely to be overcrowded. Logically, this makes some sense. A judge making decisions about admissions to a detention center that he or she also administers, compared to a judge who is not as concerned with such day-to-day administrative details, may be in a better position to know how full the center is.

Race and Ethnicity

There has been a gradual change in the racial composition of the detained youth population. The data in table 1.4 indicate a decline in the proportion of detained white youth. The decline for whites has been largely offset by a corresponding increase for black males.

Over-representation of minorities in the juvenile justice system has generated broad concern among juvenile justice professionals and policymakers across the country. The Office of Juvenile Justice and Delinquency Planning (OJJDP) has focused on this issue, mandating that states examine their own systems, that they document the patterns, examine potential causes, and develop a strategy for addressing the problem.

While minority youth were more likely to have prior court referrals and were more likely to be referred to court for more serious offenses,

> even within specific offense categories, nonwhites were often substantially more likely to be detained. For example, nonwhites were detained at a higher rate than whites when charged with drug trafficking, drug possession, motor vehicle theft, or burglary, while both groups were detained at approximately the same rate when charged with contempt of court, robbery, aggravated assault, drunkenness, simple assault, or shoplifting. (Snyder, 1990, 3)

Research on the impact of detention has found that detained youth receive more severe depositions than non-detained offenders (McCarthy & Smith, 1986; Snyder, 1990). Snyder found that "detained delinquents were five times more likely to be transferred to adult court, six times more likely to be placed out of home, and 50 percent more likely to be placed on formal probation than youth who were not detained" (1990, 3). Thus a youth's ethnic and racial background may create more opportunities for detention to take place, in turn increasing the likelihood that he or she will end up in a more restrictive and intrusive setting within the juvenile justice system.

Gender

Girls have historically been confined in detention centers for less serious offenses than have boys. In the late 1960s and early 1970s, most girls were locked up in detention centers for status offenses (Chesney-Lind & Shelden, 1992; Schwartz, 1989; Schwartz, Stekette, & Schneider, 1990). As a result, the de-institutionalization of status offender mandate in the *Juvenile Justice and Delinquency Prevention Act* (JJDPA) [42U.S.C. 5633 (a) (12) (A)] had a major impact on girls.

Currently, most girls confined in detention centers are accused of delinquent acts as opposed to status offenses. However, as can be seen in table 1.5, girls are incarcerated for far less serious delinquent behavior than is the case for their male counterparts. Based on data from the 1989 one-day count, only 23% of the girls detained were accused of Part I offenses. Sixty-two percent were accused of Part II offenses, and 15% were status offenders. In contrast, 44% of the boys were held for Part I offenses, 53% for Part II offenses, and only 3% for status offenses (Schwartz et al., 1991).

Secure Detention of Status Offenders

Although there has been a significant decrease in the proportion of girls confined in detention centers for status offenses, they are still over-represented in this area. While they accounted for only 13.8% of the total detention center population, females made up just under 50% of all status offenders in detention centers in 1989 (Schwartz et al., 1991).

In addition, there are clear differences between males and females when the types of status offenses they are detained for are compared. In 1989, the majority of female status offenders in detention centers were charged with running away (45.4%), while one-third were incarcerated for violation of valid court orders. Male status offenders are most often held for violation of valid court orders (38.1%), with runaways accounting for 33.1% (CIC, 1988).

Spending time in a detention center for violating a valid court order[1] is a phenomenon of increasing incidence. On February 2, 1987, 27.5% of all status offenders incarcerated in detention centers were charged with violations of valid court orders. In 1989, this jumped to 36.2% (CIC, 1988).

The valid court order phenomenon is, in large measure, being fueled by the numbers of youth confined for such behaviors in the state of Ohio. For example, 39% (108 youth) of all youth confined for violating a valid court order were confined in Ohio. Indiana (11%) and Utah (8%) were the second and third highest contributors out of the 23 states that held youth for violations of valid court orders (CIC, 1988).

Costs of Detention

The costs for detaining juveniles are growing. In 1979, the average expenditure per bed in publicly-operated facilities was $21,679. The average cost per bed in 1989 was $27,275, an increase of 21% after adjusting for inflation. Costs among states and the District of Columbia ranged from a low of $13,000 per bed in Indiana and Mississippi to a high of $62,276 in Connecticut, with 30 states having a cost-per-bed between $20,000 and $40,000. The differences in costs cannot be explained by regional differences among states. As can be seen in table 1.6, there are large differences in costs per bed among states within the same region (Schwartz et al., 1991).

Another way to examine a state's detention costs is to compare public juvenile detention center expenditures for youth between 10 years of age and the end of juvenile court jurisdiction (the eligible youth population). Washington, D.C., spends $183 for every eligible youth in the District, the highest of all the jurisdictions. Arkansas, at only $1.00 per eligible youth, spends the least. The majority of states (34) spend below $20 per eligible youth. States may also spend more money than is indicated by the costs of housing youth in public detention centers. Many states still detain youth in adult jails, and thus the total cost of detention is not reflected for these states in the examination of public detention facility costs (Schwartz et al., 1988).

These two methods indicate neither the value received for the money spent nor whether there are less expensive methods of accomplishing the goals of detention.

Policy Considerations

Juvenile detention is a growth industry in the United States. The number of detention centers, admissions to these centers, overcrowded facilities, and costs, are all on the increase.

There are enormous differences in the rates of admissions to detention among states that are not accounted for by serious crime variables. Instead, the differences are explained by the number of beds per 100,000 eligible youth in each jurisdiction. This suggests that secure detention is not being primarily used for the purposes it was intended to serve:

to detain youth who present a clear and substantial threat to the community and who are likely to abscond if released (Schwartz et al., 1987; Poulin et al., 1980). What little research there is strongly suggests that admissions to detention can be reduced significantly by using objective intake criteria, release with parental or guardian supervision, and other community-based alternatives (see chapters 3, 4, and 5 in this book). Moreover, this can be accomplished without jeopardizing the community and at considerably less cost (Schwartz, Barton, & Orlando, 1991). This should be good news to all elected public officials and policymakers, particularly those in states and counties experiencing fiscal problems.

The finding that approximately 50% of all juveniles confined in detention centers on any given day are being housed in overcrowded facilities is alarming. Overcrowded facilities, particularly facilities in jurisdictions with dwindling fiscal resources, will inevitably lead to deteriorating conditions of confinement, unprofessional practices, media exposés, and possible exposure to litigation. In jurisdictions with overcrowded facilities, policymakers and juvenile justice professionals would be well advised to examine their detention populations carefully and objectively. They should explore all possible options for reducing reliance on secure detention without compromising public safety before considering building larger facilities or expanding the bed capacities of existing institutions.

The practice of committing juveniles to serve time in detention should be stopped. It is costly and potentially dangerous (Schwartz et al., 1987). Instead, judges and probation workers should consider using such options as community service, restitution, and enhanced supervision. These options represent far less costly and more productive sanctions.

Conclusion

While many of the problems of juvenile detention in this country remain hidden from view, they are nonetheless real and compelling issues that must be addressed. While there are clear national definitions, standards (American Correctional Association, National Advisory Committee on Juvenile Justice and Delinquency Prevention and American Bar Association), and an overall mission for detention, they are not being adhered to in the states and in jurisdictions within states. As a result, youth who do not need to be confined for reasons of public safety are being confined in large and growing numbers.

Perhaps the most interesting thing about juvenile detention over the last two decades is the fact that little has changed: the same five states—California, Ohio, Texas, Florida, and Washington—account for the majority of youth in detention centers across the country; there are still great variations between states in admissions rates, and girls are still locked up for less serious offenses than boys.

What changes have taken place that are not for the better? More and more juveniles are being committed to serve time in detention centers; more detention centers are overcrowded, and these facilities are housing a greater proportion of the juvenile detention center populations; the problem of over-representation of minorities in the system has now reached the point where African American males make up the largest proportion of the youths confined in secure detention; and costs for secure detention are far outstripping inflation.

Because detention centers are hidden from view, the problems which confronted the system 20 years ago remain unaddressed and appear to be spiraling out of control. The use of detention consistent with recommended national standards and with practices in such enlightened jurisdictions as Broward County, Florida, and El Paso, Texas, can do much to alleviate these problems. It is time for detention to be brought out of the closet and subjected to careful and vigorous public and professional scrutiny.

Appendix: Tables

Table 1.1
Admissions and One-Day Counts, 1971–1989

| | 1971 | | 1974 | | 1977 | | 1979 | |
	No.	Rate/ 100,000	No.	Rate/ 100,000	No.	Rate/ 100,000	No.	Rate/ 100,0
Admissions	496,526	1,655	529,075	1,791	489,694	1,681	451,810	1,57
Males	349,407	2,329	371,225	2,514	375,728	2,530	356,167	2,43
Females	147,119	981	157,850	1,069	113,966	798	95,643	68
One-Day counts	11,767	39	11,010	37	9,977	34	10,683	3
Males	7,926	53	7,698	52	8,058	54	8,901	6
Females	3,841	26	3,312	22	1,919	13	1,782	1

| | 1982* | | 1984* | | 1986* | | 1988* | |
	No.	Rate/ 100,000	No.	Rate/ 100,000	No.	Rate/ 100,000	No.	Rate/ 100,0
Admissions	410,688	1,488	404,175	1,520	467,668	1,799	499,621	1,95
Males	325,461	2,311	320,952	2,363	374,461	2,823	407,288	3,11
Females	85,227	630	83,223	640	93,207	732	92,333	74
One-Day counts	13,048	47	13,772	52	16,146	62	18,014	7
Males	10,833	77	11,340	83	13,587	102	15,490	11
Females	2,215	16	2,432	19	2,559	20	2,524	2

Sources: NCCD and Hubert Humphrey Institute of Public Affairs, *Rethinking Juvenile Justice: N tional Statistical Trends*, p. 43, for years 1971 and 1974; Juvenile Detention and Correctional Facil Census, 1977, 1979, 1982–83, 1984–85, 1986–87, and 1988–89; U.S. Bureau of the Census, Current Popu tion Reports, Series P-25, published and unpublished data.

Notes: Totals pertain to all youth, including those committed to a facility (placed following adju cation), detained youth (placed pending adjudication or awaiting formal court disposition or pla ment), and voluntary admissions.

Rates are based on the numbers of youths aged 10 through the age of maximum original juven court jurisdiction for each state and the District of Columbia.

*Admissions reflect calendar years 1982, 1984, 1986, and 1988. One-day counts were taken in F 1983, 1985, 1987, and 1989.

Table 1.2

Admissions Rates, 1988

	No. of Detained Admissions	Rate/ 100,000 Eligible Youth	No. of Committed Admis- sions	Rate/ 100,000 Eligible Youth	Total No. of Admis- sions	Rate/ 100,000 Eligible Youth
Alabama	6,054	1,192	176	35	6,230	1,226
Alaska	608	881	21	30	629	912
Arizona	12,499	3,255	328	85	12,827	3,340
Arkansas	2,074	705	118	40	2,192	746
California	121,902	4,111	10,324	348	132,226	4,460
Colorado	8,237	2,340	0	0	8,237	2,340
Connecticut	2,624	1,098	0	0	2,624	1,098
Delaware	930	1,310	0	0	930	1,310
D.C.	7,685	14,779	231	444	7,916	15,223
Florida	38,300	3,257	145	12	38,445	3,269
Georgia	16,578	2,445	1,585	234	18,163	2,679
Hawaii	3,072	2,671	0	0	3,072	2,671
Idaho	679	518	152	116	831	634
Illinois	15,226	1,378	1,520	138	16,746	1,515
Indiana	10,470	1,577	1,266	191	11,736	1,767
Iowa	2,432	772	0	0	2,432	772
Kansas	3,207	1,183	21	8	3,228	1,191
Kentucky	2,605	578	101	22	2,706	600
Louisiana	3,157	670	66	14	3,223	684
Maine	nr	nr	nr	nr	nr	nr
Maryland	4,367	900	0	0	4,367	900
Massachusetts	1,749	360	1,031	212	2,780	572
Michigan	11,825	1,253	636	67	12,461	1,320
Minnesota	5,941	1,264	50	11	5,991	1,275
Mississippi	3,908	1,120	0	0	3,908	1,120
Missouri	9,321	1,914	0	0	9,321	1,914
Montana	nr	nr	nr	nr	nr	nr
Nebraska	1,901	1,062	44	25	1,945	1,087
Nevada	6,902	6,450	113	106	7,015	6,556
New Hampshire	nr	nr	nr	nr	nr	nr
New Jersey	12,495	1,539	115	14	12,610	1,553
New Mexico	5,691	1,093	0	0	5,691	3,093
New York	6,886	503	0	0	6,886	503
North Carolina	5,291	985	593	110	5,884	1,096
North Dakota	368	484	0	0	368	484
Ohio	33,305	2,654	2,929	233	36,234	2,887
Oklahoma	3,011	932	0	0	3,011	932
Oregon	6,324	2,129	93	31	6,417	2,161
Pennsylvania	12,626	994	255	20	12,881	1,014
Rhode Island	nr	nr	nr	nr	nr	nr
South Carolina	888	243	0	0	888	243
South Dakota	1,735	2,142	243	300	1,978	2,442

continued

Table 1.2
Admissions Rates, 1988 *continued*

	No. of Detained Admissions	Rate/ 100,000 Eligible Youth	No. of Committed Admis- sions	Rate/ 100,000 Eligible Youth	Total No. of Admis- sions	Rate/ 100,000 Eligibl Youth
Tennessee	15,752	2,754	0	0	15,752	2,754
Texas	25,155	1,411	156	9	25,311	1,420
Utah	5,448	2,145	588	231	6,036	2,376
Vermont	nr	0	14	31	14	31
Virginia	10,187	1,602	164	26	10,351	1,628
Washington	14,810	2,974	5,755	1,156	20,565	4,130
West Virginia	1,055	457	12	5	1,067	462
Wisconsin	4,383	793	58	10	4,441	803
Wyoming	nr	nr	nr	nr	nr	nr
Total U.S.	469,663	1,846	28,903	113	498,566	1,959

Sources: Juvenile Detention and Correctional Facility Census, 1988–89; U.S. Bureau of the Cen Current Population Reports, Series P-25, published and unpublished data.

Notes: Rates are based on the numbers of youths aged 10 through the age of maximum orig juvenile court jurisdiction for each state and the District of Columbia.

Committed youth are placed following adjudication, detained youth are placed pending adjuc tion or awaiting formal court disposition or placement.

Table 1.3
Percentage of Juveniles in Over-Capacity Facilities, 1979–1989

	1979	1983	1985	1987	1989
No. facilities	393	390	403	418	422
No. facilities over capacity	25	51	55	76	116
Percentage facilities over capacity	6.4	13.1	13.6	18.2	27.5
Total no. youths in custody	10,683	13,048	13,772	16,146	18,014
Total no. youths in custody in over-capacity facilities	938	3,604	4,288	6,233	9,066
Percentage youths in custody in over-capacity facilities	8.8	27.6	31.1	38.6	50.4

Sources: Juvenile Detention and Correctional Facility Census, 1979, 1982–83, 1984–85, 1986 1988–89.

Notes: A facility is "over capacity" when the reported juvenile one-day count on the census da greater than the facility's design capacity.

Data based on one-day counts taken on December 31, 1979; February 1, 1983; February 1, 1 February 2, 1987; and February 15, 1989.

Table 1.4

One-Day Counts by Race/Ethnicity and Gender, 1979–1989

	1979		1983		1985		1987		1989	
	No.	% Total	No.	% Total	No.	% Total	No.	% Total	No.	% Total
Males										
White/Non-Hispanic	4,109	42.9	4,361	37.7	5,541	40.2	5,717	35.4	5,544	30.3
Black/Non-Hispanic	2,576	26.9	3,553	30.7	3,861	28.0	5,339	33.1	6,999	38.3
Hispanic	1,132	11.8	1,540	13.3	1,731	12.6	2,203	13.6	2,589	14.2
Native American/Alaskan Native	93	1.0	102	0.9	97	0.7	182	1.1	355	1.9
Asian/Pacific Islander	54	0.6	90	0.8	110	0.8	146	0.9	278	1.5
Total males	7,964	83.1	9,646	83.4	11,340	82.3	13,587	84.2	15,765	86.2
Females										
White/Non-Hispanic	1,002	10.5	1,096	9.5	1,411	10.2	1,406	8.7	1,316	7.2
Black/Non-Hispanic	418	4.4	561	4.9	702	5.1	766	4.7	869	4.7
Hispanic	156	1.6	195	1.7	240	1.7	301	1.9	261	1.4
Native American/Alaskan Native	22	0.2	35	0.3	38	0.3	51	0.3	58	0.3
Asian/Pacific Islander	16	0.2	32	0.3	41	0.3	35	0.2	27	0.1
Total females	1,614	16.9	1,919	16.6	2,432	17.7	2,559	15.8	2,531	13.8
Total youth	9,578	100.0	11,565	100.0	13,772	100.0	16,146	100.0	18,296	100.0

Sources: Juvenile Detention and Correctional Facility Census, 1979, 1982–83, 1984–85, 1986–87, 1988–89.

Note: Ethnicity reported as provided; totals may be different from one-day counts presented elsewhere.

Table 1.5
One-Day Counts by Offense and Gender, 1989

| | MALE | | FEMALE | | TOTAL | |
	No.	%	No.	%	No.	%
Part I: Violent	2,284	15.9	161	7.0	2,445	14.7
Part I: Property	4,062	28.3	378	16.4	4,440	26.7
Total Part I	6,346	44.3	539	23.4	6,885	41.4
Part II	7,571	52.8	1,414	61.5	8,985	54.0
Total Parts I and II	13,917	97.1	1,953	84.9	15,870	95.4
Status Offense	417	2.9	346	15.1	763	4.6
Total	14,334	100.0	2,299	100.0	16,633	100.0

Source: Juvenile Detention and Correctional Facility Census, 1988–89.

Note: One-day count taken on February 15, 1989. Offense categories contain the following offenses: Part I Violent: murder, non-negligent manslaughter, forcible rape, robbery, aggravated assault; Part I Property: burglary, arson, larceny-theft, motor vehicle theft; Part II: all offenses not Part I or status, including probation/parole violations. A status offense is an offense not considered a crime if committed by an adult.

Table 1.6
Operating Expenditures per Bed and Total Youth by State, 1988

	Total Operating Expenditures ($)	Expenditures per Bed ($)	Expenditures per Eligible Youth ($)
Alabama	5,473,193	20,576	11
Alaska	3,314,099	48,737	48
Arizona	7,180,555	21,057	19
Arkansas	401,979	14,888	1
California	133,413,818	24,647	45
Colorado	4,644,021	26,844	13
Connecticut	3,985,648	62,276	17
Delaware	1,313,085	33,669	18
D.C.	9,541,428	36,142	183
Florida	32,894,454	23,165	28
Georgia	16,478,449	21,456	24
Hawaii	1,339,352	22,323	12
Idaho	471,043	15,701	4
Illinois	23,131,724	33,331	21
Indiana	6,529,488	13,922	10
Iowa	1,309,595	27,283	4
Kansas	3,810,406	31,753	14
Kentucky	2,864,625	35,366	6
Louisiana	5,618,515	21,445	12
Maine	nr	nr	nr

	Total Operating Expenditures ($)	Expenditures per Bed ($)	Expenditures per Eligible Youth ($)
Maryland	7,613,136	47,582	16
Massachusetts	5,065,227	55,057	10
Michigan	31,324,060	35,394	33
Minnesota	5,976,418	40,110	13
Mississippi	1,095,853	13,698	3
Missouri	6,785,218	16,155	14
Montana	nr	nr	nr
Nebraska	1,286,603	16,929	7
Nevada	7,153,570	32,079	67
New Hampshire	672,890	42,056	6
New Jersey	23,101,167	39,830	28
New Mexico	1,634,470	20,179	9
New York	23,654,090	57,135	17
North Carolina	4,723,016	25,951	9
North Dakota	289,717	24,143	4
Ohio	26,062,556	22,257	21
Oklahoma	2,265,878	24,629	7
Oregon	3,569,945	19,944	12
Pennsylvania	21,026,667	39,524	17
Rhode Island	nr	nr	nr
South Carolina	545,078	27,254	1
South Dakota	907,126	21,598	11
Tennessee	2,960,153	15,498	5
Texas	22,585,113	23,600	13
Utah	4,132,621	24,746	16
Vermont	1,150,000	38,333	26
Virginia	15,950,812	30,210	25
Washington	21,425,633	27,718	43
West Virginia	1,715,284	23,497	7
Wisconsin	5,478,885	50,730	10
Wyoming	nr	nr	nr
Total U.S.	513,866,663	27,275	35

Source: Juvenile Detention and Correctional Facility Census, 1988–89.

Notes: Expenditures provided for the preceding calendar year, coinciding with the admission year 1988. Expenditures per youth refers to the amount of money spent on detention centers for every youth in the state between the age of 10 and the end of juvenile court jurisdiction.

"nr" indicates no facilities reporting for indicated state and facility type for census year.

Notes

1. Valid court order refers to any order of a juvenile court judge to a juvenile who has been before the court and subject to a court order. In addition, the youth must receive full due process rights for the order to be valid. While status offenders are prohibited from secure detention by OJJDPA, juveniles subject to valid court orders are exempt from this prohibition, even if such orders regard such things as school attendance and other so-called status offenses.

Bibliography

Chesney-Lind, M., & Shelden, R. (1992). *Girls: Delinquency and juvenile justice.* Pacific Grove, CA: Brooks/Cole.

Krisberg, B., Litsky, P., & Schwartz, I. M. (1984). Youth in confinement: Justice by geography. *Journal of Research in Crime and Delinquency,* 21(2), 153–81.

McCarthy, B., & Smith, B. (1986). The conceptualization of discrimination in the juvenile justice process: The impact of administrative factors and screening decisions on Juvenile Court dispositions. *Criminology,* 24(1), 41–64.

Poulin, J., Levitt, J., Young, T., & Pappenfort, D. (1980). *Juveniles in detention centers and jails: An analysis of state variations during the mid 1970's.* Washington, D.C.: U.S. Department of Justice.

Schwartz, I. M. (1989). *(In)Justice for juveniles.* NY: Lexington Books.

Schwartz, I. M., Barton, W., & Orlando, F. (1991). Keeping kids out of secure detention. *Public Welfare,* Spring, 20–26.

Schwartz, I. M., Fishman, G., Hatfield, R., Krisberg, B., & Eisikovits, Z. (1987). Juvenile detention: The hidden closets revisited. *Justice Quarterly,* 4(2), 220–35.

Schwartz, I. M., Steketee, M., & Schneider, V. (1990). Federal juvenile justice policy and the incarceration of girls. *Crime & Delinquency,* 36(4), 503–20.

Schwartz, I. M., Steketee, M., & Willis, D. (1989). *Juvenile justice trends, 1977–1987.* Ann Arbor, MI: University of Michigan, Center for the Study of Youth Policy.

Schwartz, I. M., Willis, D., & Battle, J. (1991). *Juvenile arrest, detention, and incarceration trends, 1979–1989.* Ann Arbor, MI: University of Michigan, Center for the Study of Youth Policy.

Snyder, H. (1990). Growth in minority detentions attributed to drug law violators. *Juvenile Justice Bulletin, OJJDP Update on Statistics.* March.

U.S. Department of Justice, Bureau of Justice Statistics and Office of Juvenile and Delinquency Prevention. (1990). *Juvenile detention and correctional facility census, 1988–89: Public facilities* [computer file]. Washington, D.C.: U.S.

Department of the Commerce, Bureau of the Census (Producer). Ann Arbor, MI: Inter-University Consortium for Political and Social Research (Distributor).

U.S. Senate, Committee on the Judiciary. (1981). *Reauthorization of the Juvenile Justice and Delinquency Prevention Act of 1974*. Washington, D.C.: U.S. Government Printing Office.

2

Determinants of Juvenile Detention Rates

TERI K. MARTIN

Overcrowding of juvenile detention facilities threatens the security of residents and staff and undermines the quality of care which can be provided. Although facility expansion may temporarily alleviate over-crowding, the problem often returns at even more alarming levels when detainee populations once again expand without restraint. Only by understanding ways in which justice system policies and practices interact to determine the size and character of the detained population can county and state policymakers exercise continuing control over the demand for and use of secure detention space. This analysis of deten-tion rates in Cuyahoga County (Cleveland, Ohio) convincingly demon-strates the central influence of philosophy, policy, and practice on detention population levels.

Factors Affecting Use of Secure Detention

The number of juveniles admitted to a secure detention facility and their average length of stay (ALS) together determine the average daily population (ADP) of juveniles which that facility must accommodate. Two types of variables can influence the ADP of a detention facility by affecting either the number of juveniles admitted and/or their average length of stay. Determinate factors, such as county demographics and juvenile crime rates, are those that are not directly affected by the discretionary decision-making powers of juvenile justice policymakers and practitioners. Policy-based factors, on the other hand, are those that are substantially influenced by policies and practices which regulate admission to detention, court processing of detained cases, capacity of the detention facility (both physical and programmatic), and availability and use of alternatives to secure detention.

Analysis of past trends in detention use in Cuyahoga County demonstrates that policy factors have consistently had a much more powerful impact on that county's use of secure detention than have demographic "givens."

Historic Trends in Cuyahoga County's
Use of Secure Detention

Table 2.1 reveals significant fluctuations experienced in admissions, ALS, and ADPs in Cuyahoga County's secure detention facility during the past 24 years. For the most part, annual admissions and ALS show little correlation with one another, although together they clearly determine ADP.

Influence of Determinate Factors on Detention Rates

Since 1970, there has been a significant and steady decline both in the total Cuyahoga County population and in the 10–19-year-old group, as indicated in table 2.2. This decline is expected to continue at least through the year 2010, although it will become much less steep after 1990. Between 1971 and 1980, the 12–17-year-old group, from which nearly all Detention Center Admissions originate, decreased by 26%, and it was expected to decrease by a similar proportion between 1980 and 1990.

However, during this long period of steady decline in the at-risk population, the Detention Center's population has fluctuated significantly, and the 1990 ADP is presently approaching levels last observed in the late 1960s. These substantial variations in Cuyahoga County's secure detention rate (ratio of ADP to population aged 12–17, also in table 2.2), which has more than tripled since reaching its 20-year low in 1971, clearly indicates that the size of the at-risk age group in the population is not correlated with the Detention Center's ADP.

Historic data on juvenile crime rates for Cuyahoga County, the other "determinate" factor which can affect detention needs, could not be

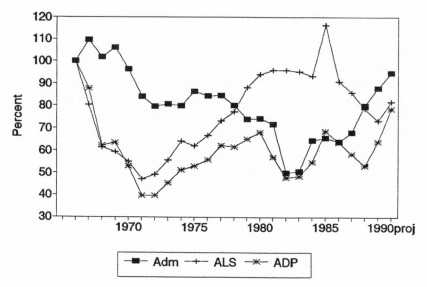

Figure 2.1. Admissions, average length of stay, and average daily population as percentage of 1966 base.

obtained for this analysis. However, it seems unlikely that juvenile crime rates have been the sole or even the most important driving force behind the historically dramatic fluctuations and recent steep rise in the County's detainee population.

Policy Factors Affecting Detention Rates

An examination of policy and resource allocation changes which have preceded or coincided with periods of significant growth or decline in Cuyahoga County's secure detention population during the past two decades illustrates that such policy changes are the most important determinants in the use of secure detention.

1966–1972

As figure 2.1 illustrates, the first and still most dramatic shift in the Detention Center's population during the past 24 years occurred between 1966 and 1971, a period of equally far-reaching changes in detention policies and practices in the Cuyahoga County Juvenile

Court. The primary impetus for these changes was extreme over-crowding of the old dormitory-style facility. While its rated capacity was then 150, its population averaged 172 and frequently was as high as 225 juveniles.

In 1973, Judge Whitlatch, then of the Cuyahoga County Juvenile Court, described the detention "control program" initiated in late 1966 as enforcement of the Court's avowed philosophy that "no child should be detained unless there was a substantial probability that he would commit an act dangerous to himself or to the community, or that he would abscond pending court disposition" (19). The cornerstone of the Court's strategy was the granting of authority to detain or release juveniles to intake referees appointed by the judges. By delegating this responsibility, the Court sought to improve promptness and consistency of intake decision-making.

Other policy and resource allocation changes designed to curb referrals to detention and to decrease average stays of detained youths were also initiated by the Court beginning in 1965. These included:

Explicitly discouraging judicial use of detention for inappropriate purposes, i.e., treatment, deterrence, or punishment.

Encouraging police to release children to parents through vigorous enforcement of detention policies which, when first implemented, resulted in the immediate release of many police-referred children.

Requiring an official complaint be filed concerning each child placed in detention, which discouraged social agencies' use of detention as preventive treatment of "pre-delinquents."

Subjecting detention placements by probation officers to the scrutiny of the intake referee, who screened out children who did not require such placement for their own or the community's protection.

Requesting assistance of state, county, and private agencies in eliminating the backlog of detained children awaiting acceptance in placements.

Expediting the clinical testing process by hiring part-time psychologists and giving detained children top priority.

Opening a new Court Annex facility, which included a detention component of 78 beds, replacing the old dormitory units which housed up to 150 juveniles.

This period of creative policy development was capped when, in 1969, Cuyahoga County's detention intake and release policy was "written almost verbatim into the law of Ohio" (Whitlatch, 1973). The resulting statute provided that "a child taken into custody shall not be detained or placed in shelter care prior to the hearing on the complaint unless his detention or care is required to protect the person and property of others or those of the child, or because the child may abscond or be removed from the jurisdiction of the court, or because he has no parents, guardian or custodian or other person able to provide supervision and care for him and return him to the court when required, or because an order for his detention or shelter care has been made by the court pursuant to this chapter" (Ohio Revised Code, Chapter 2151).

By 1971, the Court's policy and procedural initiatives had reduced the detention population by 60%, an achievement all the more remarkable since it occurred during a period when delinquency and unruly complaints rose by 25%. From figure 2.1, it is apparent that the Court's policy initiatives had a more immediate and dramatic impact on average stays than on admissions to detention, but with both reduced, the ADP plummeted to all-time lows by the early 1970s.

1972–1980

During the 1970s, the detention population increased by over 70% from the low in 1971 to a high of 117 in 1980, not because more juveniles were going in, but because they were staying much longer. This gradual but significant increase in average stays and ADP resulted primarily from a relaxation of the rigorous controls which had been instituted to combat overcrowding, as well as from a lack of capacity in alternatives to secure detention. With the betterment of conditions brought about by physical improvements and a substantially reduced population, public concern abated and the felt urgency to minimize detention use decreased. At the same time, insufficient capacity in alternatives to secure detention eroded the commitment of the Court to their use. In the absence of a mechanism to monitor detention practices, and in the face of continued individual and organizational resistance to the sweeping policy changes of the late 1960s, the initial vigilance of judges and intake referees in applying the Court's detention policies gradually lessened, until the facility again began to experience periods of overcrowding.

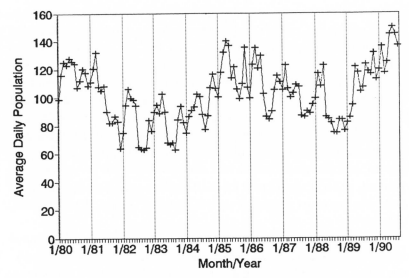

Figure 2.2. Average daily population, Cuyahoga County Detention Center.

Since 1980, the population of the Detention Center has been quite volatile. Two periods of decline, between 1980 and 1983, and from 1985 to 1988, coincide with changes in Court policy and practice which were intended to reduce the Center's population. Periods of increase, between 1983 and 1985, and from 1988 to the present, have been marked by policy and resource allocation shifts which have tended to increase admissions to secure detention. Policy changes during the past decade which have affected Cuyahoga County's use of secure detention are outlined chronologically below. Table 2.3 and figure 2.2 provide detailed pictures of average daily population trends during the 1980s.

1980–1983

In 1981, the Court established a home detention program as an alternative to secure detention, and in 1982 the first shelter care beds were made available for status offenders requiring short-term out-of-home placement. By 1983, annual admissions to these two programs totalled nearly 900, approximating the reduction in 1983 Detention Center admissions from 1980 levels. Implementation of an in-house Diversion Program in 1980 may also have contributed to the 30% reduction in the Detention Center's average population observed between 1980 and 1983.

1983–1985

The mid-decade peaking of the Detention Center's population was most likely precipitated by a change in Detention Center administration, coupled with improvements in conditions and program offerings which, taken together, rendered the secure facility a more acceptable, if not preferred, option in the eyes of judges and referees. Consent orders in a federal class-action suit, *Hanna v. Toner* (1984), mandated several enhancements. These included: implementation of a team approach for preparation of an individual care plan for each child within three days of admission; establishment of a "special treatment unit" intended to "provide a supportive, protective environment for youngsters whose emotional state demands special treatment"; enhancement of staff training requirements and opportunities; and development of a behavior-management program to "provide incentives to youngsters for appropriate social relationships."

This consent order not only resulted in enhanced treatment programming in the Detention Center, but it also provided the impetus for developing facility renovation plans, a process which may well have focused the new administration's attention more on quality and quantity of available space than on efforts to constrain the Court's need for and use of secure bedspace.

1985–1988

In 1985, with the average daily population of the Cuyahoga County Juvenile Detention Center on the rise, Juvenile Court completed plans to renovate and expand the capacity of the detention facility at a cost of approximately $5.5 million. However, following the appointment in late 1985 of a new Court Administrator firmly committed to minimizing use of secure detention, the Detention Center population began to decline, prompting a re-evaluation of the County's need for additional secure detention bedspace. In 1987, the author provided technical assistance to the Cuyahoga County Juvenile Court as it developed updated projections of detention needs.

One crucial factor in the decline in detention use between 1985 and

1988 was the development of detailed written policies and procedures intended to promote equity and consistency in detention decision-making. These policies and procedures incorporate both Ohio statutory requirements and American Correctional Association standards. By both prohibiting use of secure detention in non-delinquency cases and advocating its use only when necessary to protect the public or the juvenile or to ensure appearance for delinquency proceedings, the written policies more fully articulated the long-standing commitment of the Cuyahoga County Juvenile Court to control and minimize the use of secure detention. The written policies specify a number of basic principles which intake decision makers should follow:

1. The first priority is to release a child to his or her parents, guardian, or custodian whenever possible.
2. As the most restrictive alternative, the Detention Center should be used only as a last resort, when no other intermediate option will suffice to protect the community and the juvenile and ensure appearance at court.
3. There are a number of purposes or goals for which detention should never be used, including discipline, punishment, treatment, and administrative convenience.
4. Juveniles should also not be detained simply because more appropriate alternatives are unavailable.

Since their approval and enactment by the Court, these written guidelines have had a significant impact on decision-making by the court-appointed detention referees. However, individual judges retain discretion to remand any juvenile referred to court to secure detention.

In May of 1988, the Court Administrator, recognizing that the existence of written policies and procedures does not assure that they will be carefully and consistently practiced, assigned responsibility and authority to monitor implementation of detention policies to the individual who was then the manager of the Court's home detention and shelter care program. Figure 2.2 shows the dramatic and immediate decline in ADP which resulted from appointing this detention-use monitor. After dropping nearly 25% in one month (a month typically characterized by seasonal peaking), the Detention Center population continued to decline, stabilizing for the next year at an average count well below levels observed just before detention monitoring was implemented.

The detention monitor accomplished this reduction and control of the Detention Center's population primarily through individual case screening and tracking. He used a variety of means to accomplish population-control goals:

1. Intake decisions were screened daily to ensure that *all* admission criteria specified in the written intake policy were met in *every* case, to establish that dates were set for necessary court hearings, and to verify that time limitations specified by detention intake and court processing policies were met.
2. Transfers of detained juveniles to their final dispositions were expedited.
3. "Courtesy holds" of juveniles for other jurisdictions were limited to a maximum of 24 hours.
4. Information was provided to judges and court referees regarding the Detention Center population and home detention and shelter care openings.

In his dual role as secure detention monitor and manager of home detention and shelter care programs, this individual was ideally situated to control growth of the Detention Center population by directing his home detention and shelter care staff to maintain juveniles in the community unless secure detention was deemed essential to protect the public or ensure court appearance. He also established and administered a 24-hour emergency shelter care program for unruly juveniles apprehended on warrants and coordinated 24-hour transportation to shelters so that delinquents referred to shelter care need not spend a single night in secure detention. Assigning responsibility for secure-detention population control to the individual who managed the County's alternatives to secure detention helped to ensure that home detention and shelter care actually functioned primarily as *alternatives* to secure detention rather than as a "widening of the net" of court-ordered supervision and control.

A comparison of two "snapshot" profiles of the Detention Center population, taken by staff of Cleveland's Federation for Community Planning before (April 27, 1987) and after (August 17, 1988) detention monitoring began, demonstrates its significant impact. There were no unruly or dependency cases in the "after" snapshot, although they constituted 10% of the detention population before monitoring.

Intake monitoring reduced discretionary detentions (those remanded by judges) from 72% of the "before" population to 27% of the "after" population. The balance were juveniles remanded by judges, and therefore, according to written intake policy, *had* to be admitted to the Detention Center and held until the remanding judge agreed to their release. While 13% of the juveniles held on April 27, 1987 were awaiting post-disposition placement, only seven percent of the "after" population were awaiting placement. Finally, 39% of the "before" snapshot had been in detention over four weeks, but only one-quarter of the "after" group had been held that long. With vigilant monitoring, Cuyahoga County was clearly able to divert non-delinquent children from secure detention, to substantially reduce discretionary detentions, and to speed processing and placement of youth who must be detained.

1988 to Present

Since mid-1989, a number of significant personnel and policy changes have resulted in substantial and continuing growth both in admissions to and average stays in the Detention Center. These policy and administrative changes have diluted the effectiveness of the population-control measures which, despite significant increases in new delinquency complaints which began in 1985, had been so successful in stabilizing the Detention Center population.

One factor in the growth of the Detention Center population since 1988 has been a striking jump in the number of delinquency complaints for drug law violations. During 1989, the Court received nearly triple the number of drug violation complaints that it had had in 1988. In and of itself, the increased volume of such cases, which is probably due as much to changes in law enforcement agency and prosecutor policy as it is to greater frequency of drug offenses by juveniles, would not necessarily result in increased use of secure detention. However, early in 1989, the Court also instituted a policy of mandating secure detention for all juveniles charged with felony drug violations or commission of a crime with a firearm. This policy change has undoubtedly contributed to the significant and sustained growth in secure detention admissions and ADP which has occurred since that time.

Various changes in personnel, and the resulting shift in the Court's goals and values, have also contributed significantly to growth in the

Detention Center's population. Two new judges have been appointed to the Court since early 1989, and a new Administrative Judge took office in January 1990, replacing the judge who had filled that role since the beginning of 1985. Late in 1989, the detention population monitor left to take a new position, and in January of 1990, the Court Administrator who had appointed the monitor was dismissed by the new Administrative Judge. To date, the detention population monitor has not been replaced, and the Juvenile Court has made building a new secure detention facility one of its highest priorities.

Thirty percent more juveniles were admitted to secure detention during the first eight months of 1990 than in the correlate period in 1989, while new delinquency referrals grew by 22% during the same period. By June of 1991, the average daily population of the Center, as reported by Donna Hamparian of the Federation for Community Planning, was 140. If present trends continue unabated, it seems likely that the Detention Center ADP will once again reach levels last seen in the mid-1960s, when the general population aged 12–17 was almost twice as large. In planning for its new secure detention facility, the Cuyahoga County Juvenile Court should surely consider not only the likely impact of demographic "givens" but also the powerful impact of its own policies, practices, and resource-allocation choices on future needs for secure detention.

Managing Demand for Secure Detention

This analysis of Cuyahoga County's secure detention history suggests that the size of a jurisdiction's secure detention population is not simply something that "happens to" the locality, but rather that it is determined to a significant degree by policy choices within the control of local decision makers. A forecast of a jurisdiction's future need for secure detention bed space should not be derived simply from passive analysis of historic statistics but rather should grow out of an active understanding of the impact of changes in policies and practices on the detained population.

For jurisdictions committed to managing and controlling their use of secure detention, Cuyahoga County's experiences can be both instructive and cautionary. Detention use monitoring, which was initially so effective in Cuyahoga County, can indeed provide the cornerstone of a population-management program. However, the resistance of Cuyahoga County Juvenile Court judges to monitoring their use of secure detention has been the single most significant impediment to population-control efforts. Although some judicial resistance to a new monitoring effort is possible in any jurisdiction, judges almost always appreciate timely access to accurate information relevant to their detention admission and release decisions. Thus, to ensure that judges see detention monitoring as facilitating rather than frustrating the proper exercise of judicial discretion, a monitoring program should routinely and expeditiously provide judges with:

1. Detailed case-profile and court-processing information about detained juveniles.
2. Quantitative and qualitative descriptions of available alternatives to secure detention.
3. Trend data on average daily population, admissions, and average stay, for both secure detention and alternatives to detention.
4. Objective feedback regarding outcomes of cases admitted to secure detention and of those handled through alternate means.
5. Any other information about juveniles, the detention facility, or alternatives to detention which may be helpful in making detention and release decisions.

Other policy and program initiatives which can help to ensure that detention monitoring and population control are understood and consistently supported by local decision makers include:

1. Developing written policies and procedures which explicitly state the goals and purposes of secure detention, and which specify the principles, criteria, and processes to be applied in making intake and release decisions.
2. Formally establishing detention-use monitoring and population control as ongoing priorities by delegating to one staff member authority to review all intake and release decisions made by judges and other intake decision makers; track the court status of detained cases; expedite paperflow; arrange necessary transportation; provide regular statistical reports; and perform any other task necessary to ensure both adherence to written policies and maintenance of the Detention Center population within its bed

space capacity limits. Population control efforts are likely to be most effective if the secure detention use monitor is also closely tied to the management of alternatives to secure detention.

3. Providing for automated collection, analysis, and retrieval of case-level and aggregate data relevant to detention decision-making and monitoring.

4. Developing assessment instruments which will provide decision makers with *objective* estimates of a juvenile's risk of failure to appear and dangerousness to self or others.

5. Providing a full spectrum of alternatives to secure detention and encouraging their *appropriate* use.

6. Limiting available secure detention capacity to the minimum required to achieve the jurisdiction's stated detention goals.

Collaborative development of written detention intake and release policies by judges and court staff should help to ensure consistency of detention use over time, even if personnel and administrative structures change. Objective written criteria for placement of juveniles in secure detention and alternatives should be a part of these intake and release policies. Decision makers must continuously receive accurate and reliable information on individual cases so that decision-making criteria can be consistently applied. The systemic impact of detention decisions must also be monitored in order to improve consistency and effectiveness of detention decision-making, as well as to provide policymakers with a rational basis for making changes in their policy and practice. Finally, localities must provide the resources, i.e., staff, facilities, and programs, necessary to respond to needs generated by locally determined detention policies and practices.

The fundamental impact of court policies and their implementation on detention population levels illustrated by Cuyahoga County's experiences suggests that localities can effectively control secure detention populations at levels established by rational policy-making rather than by assuming that bed space needs will be dictated by circumstances beyond their control. One significant benefit of such efforts to control and manage secure detention use is the savings in capital and operating costs which counties can realize by avoiding unnecessary facility expansion. However, the most significant benefits can accrue to juveniles and to the public in the form of more equitable and effective detention practices.

Appendix: Tables

Table 2.1
Admissions, Average Stay, and Average Daily Population, Cuyahoga County
Detention Center, 1966–1990

Year	Admissions	Average Stay (days)	Average Daily Population
1966	4,089	15.3	172
1967	4,479	12.3	151
1968	4,165	9.4	107
1969	4,342	9.1	109
1970	3,947	8.4	91
1971	3,439	7.2	68
1972	3,258	7.5	68
1973	3,302	8.5	78
1974	3,267	9.8	88
1975	3,532	9.5	91
1976	3,449	10.2	96
1977	3,456	11.2	107
1978	3,276	11.8	106
1979	3,026	13.5	112
1980	3,037	14.4	117
1981	2,931	14.7	98
1982	2,044	14.7	82
1983	2,065	14.6	83
1984	2,633	14.3	94
1985	2,674	17.8	118
1986	2,612	13.9	109
1987	2,778	13.1	100
1988	2,770	12.0	91
1989	3,260	12.3	110
1990 (8 mos.)	2,440	13.1	133

Sources: Admissions: 1966–81 data from memorandum of March 13, 1986, R. Gallitto to Allen
Sielaff; 1982–85 data calculated by subtracting home detention admissions reported by C. Sanniti (personal communication, May 1987) from total admissions to detention reported in Annual
Reports of the Cuyahoga County Juvenile Court; 1986–87 data from Annual Reports; 1988–90
calculated from ADP and ALS data provided by J. Pokorny (personal communication, September
1990).

Average Stay: Computed from annual admissions (see above) and days of care furnished, from
Annual Reports. For 1982–87, reported total days of care were reduced by one day for each
admission to home detention (see above); 1988–90 data provided by J. Pokorny (personal communication, September 1990).

Average Daily Population: 1966–79 from R. Gallitto, memorandum; 1980–86 are annual average
4 P.M. counts from memorandum of January 6, 1987, T. Royer to R. Stepanik; 1987 is annual
average 4 P.M. count provided by C. Sanniti (personal communication, May 1988); 1988–90 data
provided by J. Pokorny (personal communication, September 1990).

Table 2.2
Detention Rates, Cuyahoga County, 1971–1990

Year	Population Aged 12–17	ADP	Detention Rate (per 100,000 pop. 12–17)
1971	201,945	68	33.7
1972	196,017	68	34.7
1973	190,089	78	41.0
1974	184,161	88	47.8
1975	178,233	91	51.0
1976	172,304	96	55.7
1977	166,376	107	64.3
1978	160,448	106	66.1
1979	154,520	112	72.5
1980	148,592	117	78.7
1981	144,896	98	67.6
1982	141,200	82	58.1
1983	137,504	83	60.4
1984	133,808	94	70.2
1985	130,112	118	90.7
1986	126,415	109	86.2
1987	122,719	100	81.5
1988	119,023	97	81.6
1989	115,327	110	95.4
1990	111,631	133	119.1
1995	110,238		
2000	109,190		

Source: 12–17 populations for 1971, 1980, 1990, and 2000 provided by R. Gallitto and J. Pokorny (personal communication, May 1987); intermediate years are interpolated.

Table 2.3

Average Daily Population, Cuyahoga County Detention Center

	1980	1981	1982	1983	1984	1985
January	98.6	111	74.9	89.7	74.4	100.1
February	116	120.7	94.4	94.7	86.5	117.8
March	125.2	132.1	106.1	88.6	90.7	132.1
April	123.1	107.7	99.6	102.4	93.2	140.1
May	128.2	104.6	98.4	89.5	102.2	136.6
June	125.8	108	94	67.7	100.5	113.7
July	124.1	89.8	64.8	66.4	88.1	121.8
August	106.9	81.8	63.2	67.7	77.1	105.7
September	112	82	62.9	63.1	86.9	98.8
October	120.4	86.8	64.4	84.3	106.5	109.8
November	117.9	82.8	83.7	93.9	116.4	135.4
December	108.3	64.1	76.1	82.2	106.4	107

	1986	1987	1988	1989	1990	
January	99.4	105.2	99.1	82.3	119.7	
February	123.6	123	116.9	85.9	136.2	
March	135	106.4	107.8	94.3	117.1	
April	120.8	100	118.6	121.6	124.8	
May	129.8	103.2	90.1	117.8	144.6	
June	102.3	108.9	84.4	103.9	150.3	
July	86.5	107.5	79.3	107.0	144.8	
August	84.5	87	74.8	123.7	136	
September	90.4	86	74.4	118.5		
October	105.4	90.2	84.1	116.6		
November	115.5	88.5	84.1	131.7		
December	111.1	95.1	76.5	112.8		

Sources: January 1980–September 1987 from memorandum of January 6, 1987, T. Royer to R. Stepanik, based on 4 P.M. counts. October–December 1987 from memorandum of August 17, 1988, C. Sanniti to A. Sielaff, based on 4 P.M. counts. January 1988–August 1990 received from J. Pokorny, based on 4 P.M. counts.

Bibliography

Cuyahoga County Juvenile Court. (1982–87). *Annual report*. Cleveland, OH.

Hanna v. Toner. (Case No. C78–1506, N.D. Ohio, final consent order, 1984).

Ohio Revised Code Ann., Chapter 2151. (1990).

Pappenfort, D. M., & Young, T. M. (1980). *Use of secure detention for juveniles and alternatives to its use*. Washington, D.C.: U.S. Department of Justice, Office of Juvenile Justice and Delinquency Prevention.

Martin, T. K. (1988). *Forecasting secure detention bedspace needs of the Cuyahoga County Juvenile Court*. Unpublished manuscript. Community Research Associates, Champaign, Illinois.

Whitlatch, W. G. (1973). Practical aspects of reducing detention home population. *Juvenile Justice, 24*, 17–25.

3

Objective Juvenile Detention Criteria: The California Experience

DAVID STEINHART

California has no rival when it comes to the confinement of children in pre-trial detention centers. According to the Children in Custody survey of the United States Department of Justice, California's rate of juvenile, pre-trial detention was the nation's highest when last measured in 1991. During that year, with about 12% of the nation's youth population, California held 30% of all juveniles confined in United States detention facilities.[1]

California has not only the highest rate of pre-trial youth incarceration but also some of the nation's most crowded youth facilities. The worst circumstances are probably those in Los Angeles County, where as many as 1,800 youths per day are jammed into detention facilities rated to hold 1,350. Overflow youth sleep on mattresses placed on dayroom floors. Other large urban counties—such as San Diego, Orange, and Fresno—also have histories of chronically over-filling their juvenile centers.[2]

California has an abundance of juvenile detention facilities, separate from adult jails, located in 45 of its 58 counties. Some of these "juvenile jails" are older, deteriorating structures badly in need of repair or replacement. This raises questions about the health and welfare of children confined under such circumstances. In San Francisco, visitors to the Youth Guidance Center find a cheerless building with water leaking from ceilings, patches of paint and plaster missing, poor heating and ventilation, and a documented asbestos problem. San Francisco recently defended a lawsuit, filed by public interest lawyers, challenging the conditions of juvenile confinement.

There is no end in sight to California's aggressive application of the power to confine minors without bail before trial. While the state's juvenile population went through a 10-year decline in the 1980s, the juvenile arrest rate held steady during that period, and California's juvenile halls therefore remained at or near capacity. Recent increases in the rates of arrest for serious and violent juvenile crimes, combined with rapid new growth of the state's juvenile population, are likely to increase referrals to detention. Inevitably, California's juvenile detention problems will intensify in the years to come unless juvenile justice administrators can institute program and policy changes to relieve the strain.

Recent interest in the reform of juvenile detention practices has been sparked in some California jurisdictions. Not surprisingly, some of the most determined efforts to control referrals to secure detention have been made in counties where facility overcrowding is a serious problem.

This chapter describes a promising and increasingly popular approach to juvenile detention control in California—the use of objective juvenile detention criteria. Four large California jurisdictions, each with a history of overcrowding, have now adopted *local* juvenile detention criteria based on models developed by the National Council on Crime and Delinquency (NCCD). In three of these counties—Los Angeles, Santa Clara, and San Francisco—the criteria were designed by NCCD and were precisely tailored to the jurisdiction's needs. The fourth county, San Diego, has implemented detention criteria borrowed from NCCD models in other jurisdictions.

This discussion is focused on the development of objective juvenile detention criteria in San Francisco. San Francisco's detention reform efforts offer an instructive example for two reasons. First, their juvenile detention criteria, the subject of public controversy, provided a display of the political and emotional forces that haunt the subject of juvenile detention. Second, of the three counties where NCCD installed juvenile detention criteria, San Francisco has the most complete follow-up data.

Detention Basics in California: Fitting Objective Criteria into the State's Juvenile Detention Scheme

Like many states, California confers upon local juvenile authorities a broad statutory power to confine minors in secure facilities after arrest and during all subsequent stages of juvenile court proceedings.[3] Statutory justifications for the continued secure detention of a minor after arrest include such trademark rationales as the minor is "likely to flee the jurisdiction of the court"; there is a need to "protect the minor" or to "protect the person or property of another"; or, the minor is "not provided with a home or suitable place of abode."[4] Status offenders and dependent and neglected youth may be detained in California but under much more restrictive circumstances, including segregation from juvenile law violators. The discussion below deals primarily with minors who have been apprehended for alleged criminal violations.

One feature of the California statutory juvenile detention scheme which is critical to understanding how the model screening criteria work is that under California law the probation officer has full authority to either release a minor after police referral or to detain him or her for further proceedings. The prosecuting attorney has no authority in this regard, and the juvenile court judge does not make the initial detention decision. Minors who are detained by the probation officer must have a judicial hearing within a very short time—generally, within 72 hours of referral. However, minors released by the probation officer before their judicial hearing deadline do not have their detention decision reviewed by the court. It is unlikely that released minors would be returned to a detention facility before trial.

NCCD detention criteria in California have been carefully adapted to this vital phase of proceedings wherein the probation officer makes the initial detain/release decision. At this critical stage, NCCD criteria act as screening standards that are more objective and restrictive than broad statutory rules. While intended to avoid unnecessary detention, the criteria are also engineered to serve public safety goals. Public safety aspects of the criteria are discussed more fully below.

NCCD's Model Juvenile Detention Criteria: How They Work

NCCD's model juvenile detention criteria were first developed and applied in a Los Angeles County pilot project in 1985. The centerpiece of the model was and is a screening instrument which awards points for specific risk factors. Every minor referred by law enforcement agencies to the probation officer is immediately rated for risk by means of a screening instrument, which consists of a point scale. Points are added up, and the minor's total score is compared to a standard risk scale used by the intake officer as a guide to the detention decision.

A copy of the screening instrument currently used in San Francisco is provided. At the bottom is a standard risk scale ("detain/release decision") which indicates that minors who score ten or more points are eligible for detention, while minors scoring nine or fewer points should be released.

The San Francisco screening instrument uses three basic risk factors: severity of offense (up to ten points), arrest history (up to five points), and probationary status (up to six points). The San Francisco instrument also has a fourth, catch-all risk factor category ("special detention cases"), and any description in this category immediately earns ten points and qualifies the youth for detention.

Risk factors and points on the screening instrument differ from county to county. In Los Angeles, for example, the screening instrument adds risk factors for "intoxication upon arrest" and "home environment," both of which are absent in the San Francisco version. In San Francisco, drug sales offenses earn seven points toward detention, while they earn five points in Los Angeles. These variations are important. They denote territorial differences in juvenile justice policy as well as distinct, local value judgments about public safety and juvenile behavior. Moreover, various screening factors and point values reflect local efforts to fine-tune each screening instrument to provide optimal control over population levels in juvenile halls.

The minor's detention screening score, and the recommendation which emerges from application of the detention scale, are advisory in nature and therefore not binding on the probation officer. This means that even if a youth scores 10 or more points and qualifies for secure detention, the probation officer may choose to release the minor to parents or to an alternative-to-detention program. Conversely, a minor who scores fewer than 10 points may be admitted to the secure juvenile facility if the probation officer believes there is some compelling reason for secure detention which is not addressed by the screening instrument or the risk score.

The retention of the intake officer's discretion is a critical feature of the NCCD model juvenile detention screening system. The screening instrument cannot, by its nature, anticipate every nuance and

SAN FRANCISCO JUVENILE DETENTION SCREENING CRITERIA

NAME OF MINOR _____ PFN _____

ADMIT DATE _____ ADMIT TIME_____ ARREST TIME _____

INSTRUCTIONS: Score each minor for each factor below and enter the appropriate score in spaces provided in the right hand column.

SCORE

1. MOST SERIOUS INSTANT OFFENSE (Score one charge only)

Serious and violent offenses
WIC 707 (b) listed offenses 10
Other listed violent offenses 7

Narcotics/Weapons Offenses
Sale of narcotics/drugs 7
Possession of firearm 10
Possession of narcotics/drugs for sale 6
Felony possession of narcotics/drugs 5
Misdemeanor possession of narcotics/drugs 3

Property offenses
Felonies 5
Misdemeanors 3

All other crimes or probation violations .... 0 _____

2. NUMBER OF PRIOR ARRESTS, LAST 12 MONTHS

Prior felony arrest within the last 7 days 5
6 or more total arrests, last 12 months 3
4 to 5 total arrests, last 12 months 2
1 to 3 total arrests, last 12 months 1
No arrests within the last 12 months .... 0 _____

3. PROBATION/PETITION STATUS

Active cases (select only one score)
With petition now pending 6
With last adjudication within 90 days 4
With last adjudication more than 90 days ago 2
Not an active case .... 0 _____

4. SPECIAL DETENTION CASES (Check whichever applies)

Escapee _____ Failed plcmt. _____ Transfer in _____ Arrest warrant _____
Bench warrant _____ Court order _____ Other (describe)_____ 10
Not applicable .... 0 _____

TOTAL SCORE _____

DETAIN - RELEASE SCALE:
Score 0-9 = RELEASE   Score 10 + = DETAIN

circumstance that may apply and be relevant in individual cases. Rather, it is designed to serve as an aggregate screening device to separate low- and high-risk youth for detention decision-making purposes. In practice, the screening instrument is a good safeguard against subjectivity and bias in the decision-making process; it anchors the detention decision in objective measures of juvenile behavior. Ultimately, however, the intake decision is left to human judgment, guided by the intake score. As we will see below, this retention of officer discretion is important in gaining support for objective criteria from probation employees.

Questions often asked about the objective screening criteria are: If you release more youth, where do they go? Also, if you release more youth, won't more crimes be committed and public safety jeopardized? The answer to the first question is that most youth are sent home without conditions, much like an adult would be released on bail or on his or her own recognizance. Youth who lack a safe or caring home environment may be referred to shelter care or foster care pending court proceedings. Youth who present a moderate level of risk—not enough to justify locked confinement but enough to suggest the need for supervision—may be referred to a "home detention" program. California law, in fact, requires each county to maintain a "home supervision" program for these youth.[5] A youth on home supervision or home detention will be allowed to stay at home, will have limits placed on freedom of movement, and will be monitored by phone or in person by a probation officer. The home supervision alternative is attractive for several reasons, not the least of which is its low cost. In San Francisco, for example, the cost of keeping a minor in juvenile hall is approximately $120 per day; the cost of home supervision is only a fraction of this secure confinement cost.

It is vitally important to monitor the subsequent performance of the youths who are released when they scored low enough on a risk-screening scale. The screening system works when youths who are released in accordance with the screening criteria perform well on release status. This means they must not commit new offenses while on release and must keep court appearance promises. Periodic monitoring of the pre-trial performance of these released youths is essential to ensure that screening criteria are being applied in a manner consistent with local public safety goals.

One benefit of the objective, point-scale screening criteria is their flexibility. If detention center populations begin to climb, the criteria can be adjusted to slow the flow of youth into secure custody. If monitoring reveals public safety problems beginning to emerge (e.g., too many new offenses are committed by youths on release status), point values and the risk scale can be changed to pull more youth at the high-risk end of the release pool into secure confinement.

Applying the NCCD Juvenile Detention Criteria in San Francisco

Troubled History of Juvenile Detention

San Francisco has a long history of problems related to juvenile detention. The detention facility itself sits on the grounds of the Youth Guidance Center (the Center), which also contains the administrative offices of the probation department and the juvenile courts. All structures at the Center are old and deteriorating. The juvenile hall units have poor lighting, heating, and ventilation and are sub-standard when measured by many modern building code requirements. In 1990, public interest lawyers sued the City and County of San Francisco, alleging improper conditions of confinement.

The rated capacity of the San Francisco juvenile hall in 1989 was 138 beds.[6] The average daily population (ADP) of the juvenile hall in 1989 was 123 youths. While the 1989 ADP was below the 138-bed limit, there were 37 days during that year when the facility held more than 138 youths. In fact, in each year between 1980 and 1989 there were some days of facility overcrowding.

San Francisco has a variety of private, non-profit youth service agencies, including some outspoken child advocacy organizations. One of the best known of these is Coleman Advocates for Children and Youth. Coleman has been among the most vocal and steadfast critics of juvenile detention practices in San Francisco and has repeatedly called for reductions in the number of detained youth. Along with other child advocates, Coleman has pointed to legal reforms prohibiting the secure detention of status offenders and to a 10-year decline in both the youth population and number of juvenile arrests as reasons to lower local detention levels. They also assert that probation officers unnecessarily detain many youths accused of petty offenses who can safely be returned to their homes.

The claims of detention policy critics are reinforced by a series of reports, produced by both city commissions and outside consultants, which have found high detention rates and inequities in the application of the power to detain. The Youth Authority's statewide juvenile hall report for 1988 noted that San Francisco's rate of juvenile detention was third highest of all 58 California counties.[7] A major concern raised by some reviewers of San Francisco's juvenile detention policy is the disproportionately high rate of pre-trial confinement for African-American youths relative to their representation in the county youth population.

In 1986, after the suicide of a young man in the juvenile hall, San Francisco hired Jefferson Associates to draft a new juvenile justice plan for the city. In 1987, the Jefferson team issued a report calling for new and more restrictive juvenile detention criteria and the creation of a network of community services to serve as alternatives to youth detention. The report concluded that if alternatives were established, San Francisco would need less than half its present secure detention capacity. The Jefferson recommendations were adopted by the city and county supervisors and thus became official policy.

Tailoring the Objective Detention
Criteria to San Francisco's Needs

In 1988, NCCD was invited to help the Probation Department analyze its detention criteria as a start toward realizing certain objectives of the Jefferson Plan. NCCD's initial study of the flow of youth into secure detention quickly confirmed the need for more restrictive intake criteria. Of 538 youths referred to the probation officer for law violations in a 1988 study cohort, we found that more than three-fourths were securely detained in the juvenile hall for at least one day, and more than half were highly likely to be placed in secure confinement after three days. Moreover, NCCD found that youths were highly likely to be placed in secure confinement regardless of offense severity and even for low-level offenses such as trespassing or vandalism.

NCCD recommended that San Francisco adopt point-scale criteria for detention modeled on the intake screening systems which NCCD had already installed in Los Angeles and Santa Clara counties. The city and county acted upon this recommendation by adopting, with minor modifications, the Santa Clara County detention screening instrument and putting it into effect for all youths referred to the San Francisco Youth Guidance Center.

Subsequently, NCCD was retained under contract with the city and county to fine tune the new detention screening system. The fine tuning was necessary because, after several months of application, it was clear that the screening instrument borrowed from the sister Bay Area county was not having the desired effect of reducing population levels in the San Francisco juvenile hall.

The failure of the "borrowed" criteria to impact San Francisco detention levels was not surprising to NCCD. Based on prior experience, we knew that it was vitally important to develop local criteria in a careful and measured fashion. Detention risk factors, points, and other details must be tailored to produce a close fit with local practice, procedure, and juvenile justice policy. It would not, in NCCD's view, suffice to copy-cat the criteria from another jurisdiction.

The NCCD approach to tailoring local, objective detention criteria begins with a thorough analysis of the characteristics of the detained juvenile population. At a minimum, it is desirable to analyze the following features for each member of a representative group of detainees: age, gender, referral offense, length of stay (broken down by pre- and post-dispositional time in the facility), arrest history, probation history, and special status items, such as whether the youth was the subject of a bench warrant, an escape from custody, or a failure in private placement.

Moreover, some jurisdictions consider other characteristics to be important indicators of risk related to release, such as family cohesiveness and drug or alcohol intoxication upon referral. Both of these latter characteristics are highlighted as separate risk factors on the Los Angeles County juvenile screening instrument.

To determine with precision what San Francisco's juvenile detention criteria should be, NCCD examined a new sample of 382 youths referred to the Juvenile Probation Department for public offenses during a five-week period in May-June, 1989. We found that three-fourths of all referred youths were being detained in the juvenile hall for more than 24 hours *even though the Department was then using point-scale criteria borrowed from another county.* As in the 1988 review, we found that youths were likely to be securely detained regardless of their referral offense. Clearly, the point-scale criteria were doing little more than providing an appearance of controlling admissions to detention and were already in need of an overhaul.

Based on our findings, NCCD recommended a number of revisions in risk factors, points, and detention procedures. As an interim goal, NCCD proposed that the Juvenile Probation Department adopt a target of reducing the secure detention rate from 76% to 60% of referrals. This was offered as an interim objective because we believed that once the system began to demonstrate its effectiveness in both reducing detention and maintaining public safety, we could consider more substantial cuts in the detention rate.

Juvenile Justice Management Issues Related to the Adoption of Objective Juvenile Detention Criteria

Wherever NCCD worked to implement objective juvenile screening criteria in California, we encountered initial skepticism and resistance. This reaction became predictable as we began to repeat the experience in new jurisdictions. Most of the resistance came from line staff, more specifically, from probation officers who were either cool or openly hostile to the idea of having their unbridled discretion tethered to an objective and numerical rating system. Though not every line worker was hostile to the concept, many perceived the application of new detention technology and the use of points instead of value judgments as attacks on their authority and their professional self-esteem.

By contrast, supervisors and high-level managers tended to welcome new criteria because they promised much needed benefits, including control over the flow of youth into detention, control over the significant costs of operating detention centers at or beyond capacity, and as a reliable and objective system that would lend fairness and predictability to the detention process.

The resistance of line staff was perhaps most intense when NCCD introduced model detention criteria at the Santa Clara County Probation Department in 1986. At the time, Santa Clara County had a large juvenile hall (329 beds) in its major city of Santa Jose, high population levels in the hall, and a strong and vocal local probation union. The union newsletter suggested that NCCD's hidden agenda was to "privatize" the county's juvenile justice system by causing the referral of large numbers of youth to private youth service organizations in the community. The union leader asserted that NCCD had failed to involve the union in the planning phases of the project, and he confronted NCCD's staff by inviting them as profanely as possible to "get out of town." In other counties, the initial resistance was more polite or subtle but unmistakably present.

NCCD believed that it was vital to deal with these points of resistance. To do so, we convened meetings to train personnel in the use of criteria and to air probation staff concerns. In each of these meetings, we underscored that the point-rating system was advisory in nature and that intake officers would retain their discretion—the power to override the recommendation of the detention scale when there were compelling reasons to do so. When driven home repeatedly, the fact that individual discretion was to be retained seemed to have a calming effect. Even where doubts remained, the process of inviting staff into open discussion of their fears and concerns had an ameliorative effect that smoothed the path toward implementing the new screening system.

We also learned that once new criteria were put into effect, the skepticism of line workers often evaporated and a growing trust and reliance on the new intake rating system developed. Once probation officers had a chance to get familiar with the system, most found that it did indeed help focus, organize, and clarify the elements of evaluation that entered into their detention decisions. Moreover, the intake form became a part of the case file, providing uniform documentation of the reasons for detention or release of the minor in lieu of no record at all. This backup documentation sometimes proved helpful to probation staff who could, if asked, justify their decision on objective grounds recorded on the intake screening form.

Even though experience tells us that most often system-wide confidence in objective detention criteria tends to grow and stabilize, not everyone remains pleased. In San Francisco, one of the two probation officer unions has challenged the criteria as too liberally oriented in favor of release. In fact, this small band of probation employees maligned the detention criteria in a public campaign against a 1990 bond measure to replace the dilapidated 138-bed juvenile hall with a smaller, more modern detention facility. This is discussed below in relation to public safety issues.

Controlling Overrides

When a probation officer goes against the recommendation of the objective risk score by deciding to detain a low-scoring minor or by deciding to release a high-scoring minor, the decision is called an "override" of the criteria. It is important to allow overrides for the reasons discussed above. However, it is also critically important to monitor and control the number of overrides in order to maintain the integrity of the objective screening criteria and to avoid a dilution of their effect (which often results in new and higher levels of detained youth).

Override performance was poor when it was first measured in each of the three counties NCCD helped to install objective juvenile detention criteria. In early monitoring studies in San Francisco, for example, in excess of 50% of the youths who qualified for release based on their score alone consistently had that qualification overridden in favor of detention. This means that more than half of referred youth in San Francisco who scored nine or fewer points were nevertheless detained because the probation officer ignored or "overrode" the score. NCCD has recommended that overrides be kept within a range that does not exceed 10% to 15% of youths whose risk scores are within the release zone. This is a difficult override target for most counties. It generally cannot be achieved unless supervising probation personnel review each override decision made by an intake officer to confirm the basis and compelling need for override in favor of secure detention.

Most overrides resulting in continued secure detention of the minor come about not because the probation officer is trying to sabotage the screening system by locking up as many youths as possible, but rather because there is some practical impediment to the desired release of such youths. Most often in these cases there is some problem with the parents. Sometimes they cannot be located within the 24-hour grace period (the period which does not yet count as a secure detention), and the minor is held over until the parents can be found. At other times, parents are found but refuse to come to the facility to retrieve their child either because they want to "teach the kid a lesson" by having him or her confined for a longer period or because they find it convenient to have the child safely supervised and detained while they pursue other activities.

NCCD recommended several measures to speed the return of low-risk children to their parents. The city was urged to adopt a policy statement that "secure detention in the juvenile hall should be reserved for youth who pose a measurable public safety risk," and that "scarce and costly detention beds should not be occupied by lower risk youth whose parents are uncooperative." Another recommendation was to assign additional probation staff to the task of locating hard-to-find parents. Where parents had genuine transportation problems, transport by probation officers was recommended as a cost-effective alternative to the expense of multiple-day occupancy of a juvenile detention bed. Finally, probation staff was advised to be firm with parents who sought to use the probation department as a baby-sitting service and to remind these parents that they could be billed for the cost of juvenile hall confinement. While these inducements to swift retrieval of low-risk youth can improve the overall performance of the detention screening system by reducing overrides, they do not work in every case. Overrides resulting in higher detention levels need continued monitoring at the supervisory levels of responsible agencies.

Effect of the New Detention Criteria on Juvenile Hall Population Levels in San Francisco

The ADP of the San Francisco juvenile hall in 1989 was 123 youths, with 37 days of overcrowding. In 1990, the ADP dropped to 109 with no days of overcrowding. In 1991, the ADP fell to 94—the lowest level in 10 years—with no days of overcrowding.

This significant downward trend in the detained juvenile population is due in part to the steady application of the new detention criteria after they were re-designed by NCCD and re-implemented in January of 1990. However, the direct effect of the new detention criteria on juvenile hall populations in San Francisco cannot be determined with precision because many other significant factors have intervened. Among these other factors are the hiring of a new Chief Juvenile Probation Officer committed in principle to expansion of alternatives to pre-trial juvenile detention; a city and county charter amendment which transferred management responsibility for the Juvenile Probation Department from the Superior Court to the Executive Branch of government under a new Juvenile Probation Commission; the temporary decertification of the Youth Guidance Center as a suitable place for the confinement of minors by the California Youth Authority; the aggressive pursuit of detention reform policies by local advocacy groups; a 1990 NCCD study concluding that San Francisco should plan to replace the existing detention center with a facility having 72 rather than 138 beds; and the expansion of the home detention program to supervise minors on release who would otherwise be confined in the juvenile hall.

While the impact of objective detention criteria adopted in San Francisco cannot be separated from other factors affecting population levels, it is clear that the new juvenile screening system in San Francisco has made an important contribution to the present results. The first and boldest step taken by the city and county to control unacceptably high levels of youth detention was the adoption of NCCD model juvenile detention criteria. As criteria began to have the desired effect of identifying low-risk youths who could safely be released, juvenile justice administrators turned their attention to other key components of a successful system for the pre-trial supervision and control of arrested youth. These other key components included the expanded use of both home detention in lieu of incarceration in a public facility and the involvement-based agencies and neighborhood groups in the development of new programs to serve high-risk youth. In policy terms, the objective risk criteria have served as the nucleus for a new juvenile detention policy in San Francisco, with a restored emphasis on 21 services designed to prevent the escalation of youth behavior problems into serious and violent juvenile crime. While some features of this new policy have yet to be implemented, there is strong community-wide support for the new policy direction.

Public Safety Issues

Of paramount concern to all juvenile justice decision makers is the public safety impact of each decision to release an arrested youth before court proceedings. In 1990, San Francisco's juvenile detention criteria were attacked in the press and other media on the public safety issue. The attack arose in the context of a November 1990 local ballot measure that would have supplied funds to rebuild the Youth Guidance Center with approximately 72 juvenile detention beds instead of the present 138 beds.

The proposal to build a smaller juvenile hall was founded on a study conducted by NCCD after it was hired by the city and county to evaluate juvenile detention bedspace needs to the year 2009. The NCCD study showed that, based on available demographic data, San Francisco's at-risk juvenile population (ages 10–17) would decline in the coming decades. Moreover, the report offered a bed-savings plan which, if adopted, would avoid the need to build 65 costly detention beds. The combined effect of these factors—the lower juvenile population and the adoption of a reasonable bed savings plan—led to the NCCD recommendation that 72 secure beds would be adequate to serve San Francisco's needs over the next 20 years.

When published in March 1990, the NCCD report was assailed by one of two local probation unions. These officers agreed that San Francisco needed a new Youth Guidance Center, but they wanted more detention beds, not fewer than the present number. They focused their attack on the public safety issue challenging the point-scale detention criteria which had then been in effect, in one form or another, for more than a year. They asserted, in press articles and elsewhere, that detention criteria had resulted in the release of dangerous young criminals into the community. They recruited to their cause a celebrated political antagonist of the current San Francisco mayor. The antagonist pilloried the objective juvenile detention criteria in a local newspaper as follows:

In fact, the current mayoral administration already has weakened the standards for defining juvenile offenders. The intake officers at juvenile hall use a set of "Juvenile Detention Screening Criteria" to determine whether a juvenile should be detained pending a hearing on his or her arrest. . . . [Because of changes in the points awarded for narcotics and firearms charges], a 17 year old with 10 prior arrests who was arrested for selling crack cocaine and carrying a loaded .357 magnum would immediately be released. . . . These dangerous new release policies only came to light last month in the debate over the juvenile hall bond measure.[8]

In the heat of this campaign for and against the Youth Guidance Center bond measure, the opponents grossly exaggerated the operational features of the intake screening system. A prime example of this distortion was the assertion by the Mayor's adversary that a 17-year-old minor with 10 priors arrested with a loaded gun for selling cocaine would automatically be released. In truth, such a minor would earn ample points on the San Francisco risk instrument and would be detained unless the probation officer had some compelling reason to override the score in favor of release.

Politically driven rhetoric reveals little about the public safety consequences of using objective juvenile detention criteria. The most reasonable and reliable means of testing the safety of release criteria is to track the follow-up performance of minors released according to the criteria. Even before the war of rhetoric began on the Youth Guidance Center bond measure in 1990, NCCD had taken steps to conduct the necessary evaluation.

NCCD studied a sample of 227 youths referred to the Juvenile Probation Department for public offenses during a three-week period in January and February 1990. Each released youth was tracked for 30 post-release days to measure success or failure on release. A 30-day period was selected because California law requires an adjudication hearing (trial) for non-detained youth within 30 days of filing a petition. If, upon trial, the minor is deemed to come within the jurisdiction of the Juvenile Court, the court then takes over as prime decision maker on future confinement, and the release decision made by the probation officer at intake is no longer relevant to the case.

Failure on release was defined as a failure to appear at a scheduled court hearing within 30 days or a re-arrest and referral to probation within 30 days. A re-arrest/referral measure, rather than a re-adjudication ("guilty as charged") standard, was used because the court data system made it extremely difficult to link adjudications to individual arrest incidents.

The results of the follow-up study were as follows:

Only three of all youth released in accordance with the detention criteria (those scoring nine or fewer points at intake) were re-arrested during the follow-up period (a 94% success rate).

The severity of re-arrest offenses was low for all youth scoring nine or fewer points and released at intake. Re-arrest offenses in this low-risk group included one charge of drug possession, one charge of vehicle theft, and one charge of receiving stolen property.

All released youth were 100% successful in making scheduled court appearances; there were no failures to appear.

How do these release performance results compare with other state and national groups? There are no accepted national or state standards for juvenile, pre-trial release performance. Some studies of juveniles on pre-trial release have been conducted in various states to test the safety impact of detention criteria. Comparison of the San Francisco results with those studies is speculative because the other juvenile release studies involve different detention criteria, youth samples, and follow-up periods. Such studies provide only a general basis of comparison, not a formal reference standard. Nevertheless, with these limitations in mind, NCCD compared the performance of youth in the San Francisco release group with other studies because it was the only comparison available.

Compared to these other study groups, the San Francisco minors released in accordance with the model detention criteria had excellent overall performance while on pre-trial release status. Table 3.1 compares the pre-trial arrest performance of the San Francisco study group with the performance of 10 other study groups of juveniles and adults on pre-trial release. The San Francisco success rate of 94% is the second-best of all 11 groups in the comparison sample. Table 3.2 compares court appearance rates of the San Francisco study group with the appearance rates of 11 other study groups of juveniles and adults on pre-trial release. The San Francisco success rate of 100% is equal to that of the best-performing groups in the comparison sample.[9]

This follow-up study of youth released in accordance with the San Francisco juvenile detention criteria supports the conclusion that the criteria are working well to meet community public safety goals. Though the public safety results of this evaluation are excellent, there is a continuing need to monitor objective juvenile detention criteria in San Francisco and wherever they are applied. If points or risk factors on the form are adjusted, there is a renewed need to monitor the public safety impact of the changes made.

The Need for Continued Monitoring of
Objective Detention Criteria

The objective juvenile screening criteria have other monitoring requirements above and beyond the need to conduct periodic checks of their public safety impact. The intake criteria are really part of a screening system which, like any machinery, needs regular maintenance. The first maintenance requirement is to make sure that the intake form is being uniformly applied to all referred youth and that forms are being properly scored to completion; this is especially applicable in a large jurisdiction with high referral volume. Another need previously mentioned is the need to monitor and control overrides to ensure that system integrity is not being violated by frequent decisions to ignore the objective screening score. Periodically, samples of youths should be evaluated to determine the true detention rate, i.e., percentage defined and released. These same samples can serve as a supply of released youths to be followed for pre-trial violations and failures to appear as a public safety test. While these monitoring points appear to impose a large work requirement, they are in fact quite simple to perform. Unless there are frequent changes in the points and risk factors, samples taken twice per year on a one- to three-week flow of youths should suffice to keep the system operating at efficient levels.

Appendix: Tables

Table 3.1
Success Rates (No Re-Arrests) Among Pre-Trial Release Groups
of Juveniles and Adults

	Year	Success Criteria	% Success
Juveniles, Broward Co., FL, detained at home	1990	No re-admission to secure facility from home detention	95
Juveniles, San Francisco, CA, pre-trial release	1990	No re-arrest, 30 days	94
Juveniles, Los Angeles Co., CA, pre-trial release	1987	No re-arrest, 30 days	91
Juveniles, Arapahoe Co., CO, pre-trial release	1984	No re-detention, 90 days	91
Juveniles, Taos Co., NM, pre-trial release	1980	No re-arrest, 80 days	91
Adults, State of California, bail bond	1981	No re-arrest before trial	91
Juveniles, Louisville, KY, pre-trial release	1983	No re-arrest, 80 days	90
Adults, Miami, Milwaukee, Portland, supervised release	1985	No re-arrest before trial	88
Adults, State of California, 10% bail	1981	No re-arrest before trial	88
Juveniles, Gloucester Co., NJ, pre-trial release	1980	No re-arrest, 80 days	87
Juveniles, Los Angeles Co., CA, pre-trial release	1989	No re-arrest, 30 days	82

Sources: See bibliography.

Table 3.2
Court Appearance Success Rates (No Re-Arrests)
Among Pre-Trial Release Groups of Juveniles and Adults

	Year	Success Criteria	% Success
Juveniles, San Francisco CA, pre-trial release	1990	No FTA,* 30 days	100
Juveniles, Los Angeles Co., two release groups	1987 1989	No FTA, 30 days	100**
Juveniles, Taos Co., NM, pre-trial release	1980	No FTA, 80 days	100
Juveniles, Gloucester Co., NJ, pre-trial release	1980	No FTA, 80 days	97
Juveniles, Broward Co., FL, detained at home	1990	No FTA while on home detention	94
Juveniles, Louisville, KY, pre-trial release	1983	FTA, 80 days	91
Adults, Milwaukee, Portland, supervised release	1985	No FTA before trial	86
Adults, State of California, bail bond	1981	No FTA before trial	83
Adults, State of California, 10% bail	1981	No FTA before trial	77
Adults, 11,000 U.S. felony defendants on bail	1988	No FTA before	76
Juveniles, Arapahoe Co., CO, pre-trial release	1984	No FTA, 90 days	72

Sources: See bibliography.

*FTA = Failure to appear.

**L.A. figure inconclusive owing to court data limitations.

Notes

1. The Children in Custody Survey for 1989 found that, on a single counting day, there were 18,014 juveniles confined in detention facilities nationwide, of which 5,589 (32%) were confined in detention facilities in California.

2. More recently (1991), detention population levels in Los Angeles County juvenile halls have abated somewhat owing to the aggressive revisions of the NCCD detention criteria, to accelerated case-processing programs that have cut length of stay in detention, and to cuts in county probation funds, which have made it impossible to support the expense of operating all facilities at overpopulated levels.

3. While California makes liberal use of the power to hold minors in juvenile facilities before trial, the state has very strict rules prohibiting the confinement of children in adult jails and police lockups after arrest. The jail-removal law, drafted by NCCD and signed into law in 1986, brought California into compliance with federal Juvenile Justice and Delinquency Prevention Act (JJDPA) requirements on the confinement of juveniles in adult jails.

4. California Welfare and Institutions Code, Section 628.

5. California Welfare and Institutions Code, Sections 628.1, 636.

6. Capacity ratings are determined by the California Youth Authority, which has a statutory obligation to set standards for juvenile hall operations and to inspect youth detention facilities in California.

7. *California Juvenile Hall Population Summary Report No. 21, Calendar Year 1988.* Sacramento, CA: California Youth Authority, August 1989, p. 38. San Francisco's admission-to-detention rate for 1989 was 1,086.6 youths per 10,000 in the eligible county youth population, exceeded only by Del Norte and Kings counties in that year.

8. "Proposition B is Crime," by State Senator Quentin Kopp, in the *San Francisco Independent*, September 25, 1990, p. 11.

9. It is important to note, as stated in the text, that the comparisons are imperfect owing to differences in state laws, follow-up periods, performance standards, size of study groups, and other factors. The limitations of the comparisons, as well as additional information and citations for each of the studies used in the comparison, are covered more thoroughly in the NCCD report entitled *Testing the Public Safety Impact of Juvenile Detention Criteria Applied at San Francisco's Youth Guidance Center*, by David Steinhart, San Francisco, September 1990 (24 pages).

Bibliography

Austin, James, & Krisberg, Barry. (1985). Evaluation of the field test of supervised pretrial release. San Francisco: National Council on Crime and Delinquency.

Community Research Center. (1983). A community response to a crisis: The effective use of detention and alternatives to detention in Jefferson County, Kentucky. Prepared for the U.S. Department of Justice. Office of Juvenile Justice and Delinquency Prevention. Champaign: University of Illinois.

————. (1984). The Arapahoe detention alternatives program. Prepared for the U.S. Department of Justice. Office of Juvenile Justice and Delinquency Prevention. Champaign: University of Illinois.

Kihm, Robert C. (1980). Prohibiting secure juvenile detention: Assessing the effectiveness of national standards detention criteria. Prepared for the U.S. Department of Justice. Office of Juvenile Justice and Delinquency Prevention. Champaign: University of Illinois.

Krisberg, Barry, and Austin, James. (1983). Evaluation of Bail Reform Act of 1979 (AB 2). San Francisco: National Council on Crime and Delinquency.

Orlando, Judge Frank, Schwartz, Ira M., and Barton, William H. (1990). Broward County Juvenile Detention Project: Summary of results. Ann Arbor: University of Michigan, Center for the Study of Youth Policy, 1990.

Steinhart, David. (1987). Failure analysis for juveniles released during test of detention screening criteria in Los Angeles County. San Francisco: National Council on Crime and Delinquency.

Steinhart, David, & Steele, Patricia A. (1989). Follow-up study of minors released from probation custody in Los Angeles County using juvenile detention criteria. San Francisco: National Council on Crime and Delinquency.

U.S. Department of Justice. (1988). Felony defendants in large urban counties. Washington, D.C.: U.S. Bureau of Justice Statistics.

4

Reducing the Use of
Secure Detention in
Broward County, Florida

WILLIAM H. BARTON, IRA M. SCHWARTZ,
AND FRANKLIN A. ORLANDO

In the late 1980s, Florida faced a crisis in juvenile detention, one that had been building steadily since the beginning of the 1980s. More than 1,500 youths were confined in Florida's secure detention facilities on any given day, the state's rate of detention (121 per 100,000) was twice the national average and exceeded by only three states, only 46% of the detained youths were charged with Part I felonies, and detention costs accounted for 40% of the state's overall delinquency budget (Orlando and Barton, 1989). Many of its detention centers were overcrowded, and conditions inside several of the facilities were abominable.

In early 1988, a class-action lawsuit had been brought against the Broward Regional Detention Center in Fort Lauderdale, Florida for chronic overcrowding and unsafe conditions. With funding from the Annie E. Casey Foundation and Florida's Department of Health and Rehabilitation Services (HRS, the agency responsible for the operation of the Detention Center), the Center for the Study of Youth Policy at the University of Michigan and Florida Atlantic University initiated a two-year Detention Project. The Project's goals were relatively clear and straightforward—to reduce the use of secure detention for low-risk youths by introducing more objective intake screening procedures and developing alternative programs.

This chapter discusses the context, process, and outcomes of implementation of the Broward County Detention Project. What did the project accomplish? How was the project able to achieve what it did?

What prevented it from being even more successful? How stable do the changes appear to be?

The Broward Detention Project

The Center for the Study of Youth Policy selected Broward County as the site for a detention initiative for two primary reasons: first, its detention center was the target of the class-action lawsuit mentioned above; and second, it was the home community of Judge Frank Orlando (Ret.), the Director of the Center for the Study of Youth Policy at Florida Atlantic University in Fort Lauderdale. The lawsuit provided the jurisdiction with the impetus to consider changes, and the presence of Judge Orlando provided an on-site person with considerable expertise and local political influence to oversee the project. The Casey Foundation's commitment to fund both the implementation and evaluation of the project provided fiscal leverage to influence local program and policy decisions. Beginning in 1988, the project's two-year strategy was to analyze Broward's existing detention practices, facilitate the development of detention alternatives, effect necessary policy changes, and encourage the development of mechanisms to sustain the changes.

The ideological and inter-organizational environment of juvenile justice in Broward County could best be described as contentious. Primary responsibility for operating detention programs, as well as all other juvenile justice programs, rested with the state's Department of Health and Rehabilitative Services (HRS). HRS is a mammoth human services umbrella agency with an unusual mix of centralized (state-level policy and planning authority) and decentralized (district-level operational autonomy) functions. Other agencies, including the Court, the State Attorney's Office, police and sheriff's departments, and the Public Defender's Office, all maintained varying levels of interest in detention matters. As could be expected, it proved difficult to develop a working consensus among these parties regarding detention policies and practices. Project staff hoped that the availability of foundation funds would be the "carrot," pressure from the lawsuit the "stick," and their own efforts, especially those of Judge Orlando, the requisite catalyst for change.

At the conclusion of the project in the middle of 1990, Broward's detention center was less overcrowded, a fledgling network of alternatives was tenuously in place and being utilized without jeopardizing public safety concerns, a precarious cease-fire between the many relevant agencies was in effect, and detention intake practices had become somewhat more consistent and controlled.

Detention in Florida and Broward County during the 1980s

To place the Project's efforts and achievements in the proper context, one must understand how juvenile detention was structured by Florida statutes. It is also useful to take a somewhat longer, historical look at the state's use of juvenile detention to appreciate the balance of forces that affected detention practices. From this framework, one can get a better sense of what the Project faced when it began in 1988.

Juvenile detention in many jurisdictions is attached to and operated by the juvenile court, usually at the county level. Intake staff screen referrals from the police and accept remands from the court. Florida's detention scenario was a bit more complicated than most. Detention centers were and still are operated by the state's Department of Health and Rehabilitative Services (HRS), with one or more facilities in each of its 11 districts. In 1988, four distinct agencies had a voice in intake decisions: law enforcement, HRS, state prosecuting attorneys, and the court. The existing statutes provided HRS with little power to affect intake decisions. As in most jurisdictions, the Court could detain a youth for a wide variety of reasons. Cases brought in from the street by the police were subject to screening by HRS detention intake staff. For each such case, the police and intake worker each made a recommendation regarding detention. If they disagreed, they contacted the State Attorney's Office for a decision.[1] All youths initially detained were to receive a detention hearing within 24 hours, at which time a judge would review the case and decide whether or not detention should be continued. Of the four agencies involved, only HRS had an obvious stake in limiting the detention population, since it operated the facilities. The interests of the police, prosecutors, and court were best served by decisions to detain. Is it any wonder, then, that Florida had such a high rate of juvenile detention?

1980 Statewide Detention Reform Attempt

In 1980, following some national interest in developing standards for juvenile justice policies and programs, a coalition of advocates succeeded in changing Florida's detention statutes to restrict the use of detention. As a result, the state experienced a 21% reduction in detention admissions and a 16% reduction in the average daily population in secure detention between fiscal years 1979–80 and 1980–81.[2] Moreover, these reductions were accompanied by neither increases in law violations committed by released youths prior to their hearings, dramatic increases in the numbers of youths failing to appear for court hearings, nor increases in the rate of transfers to the adult system (Florida Department of HRS, 1981; McNeese & Ezell, 1983). In simple terms, the new detention policy "worked." Despite these results, the legislation was overturned during the following session, and the detention rates skyrocketed immediately. Secure detention admissions increased by 47%, and the average daily population rose by 62% (McNeese & Ezell, 1983).

The policy reversal was engineered by a powerful coalition of police, judges, and state attorneys, assisted by a series of sensationalistic newspaper articles. According to McNeese and Ezell (1983), the reform coalition failed by underestimating the extent to which the use of juvenile detention allowed the court, police, and prosecutors to demonstrate a symbolic ability to control juvenile crime and protect the public. In such a context, the objective effects of detention policies were essentially irrelevant. These authors recommend that those who would reform juvenile detention in conservative states would do better to concentrate on pragmatic strategies (e.g., cost effectiveness) rather than value-based strategies (e.g., protection of children's due process rights), to focus on bureaucratic rather than legislative change, and to decentralize the effort, choosing a progressive local arena rather than an entire state.

Patterns of Detention Use: 1982–1988

Florida's use of detention continued to escalate during the mid-1980s, and Broward County was no exception. Table 4.1 presents a year-by-year comparison of secure and home detention use in Broward and the rest of the state from fiscal year 1982–83 to fiscal year 1990–91.

For each year, the total admissions, direct admissions, average daily population (ADP), and average length of stay (LOS) are shown. Total admissions include both direct admissions and transfers.

By the middle of 1988, the number of direct admissions to secure detention in Broward had risen 37% from fiscal year 1982–83, while the average daily population had increased from 82.7 to 160.9, a 95% rise. The rest of Florida also saw a 37% increase in direct admissions to secure detention but only a 50% rise in the ADP over the same period. Broward's higher ADP increase was the result of a longer average length of stay for cases securely detained (16.1 days compared to 14 days statewide in FY 1987–88).

To relieve some of the pressure from the escalating use of secure detention, home detention became increasingly utilized in many jurisdictions. Note the small number of direct admissions to home detention. Most of the home detention admissions were court-ordered transfers from secure detention, clearly an option for dealing with overcrowded facilities, albeit under the control of the court. The use of home detention effectively doubled, both in Broward and the rest of the state, by FY 1987–88. Interestingly, the average length of stay for home detention cases was much longer than for secure detention cases (e.g., for FY 1987–88: 32.9 days v. 16.1 days in Broward; 23.4 days v. 14.0 days in the rest of the state). Although both secure and home detention reflect the same legal status and are subject to the same statutory timelines, there is clearly less pressure to move cases out of home detention than out of secure detention.

Increase in Cases Referred to the
Department of Health and Rehabilitative Services

Much of the increase in detention use in the 1980s can be attributed to a rise in the number of delinquency cases referred to HRS and the state's attempt to continue detaining at the same rate.[3] Table 4.2 shows the population of youths aged 10 to 17, the number of delinquency cases referred to HRS, and the number of felony cases referred to HRS for each year in Broward and the rest of the state. Table 4.2 also shows the rate of referrals per 1,000 youths in the population. Cases referred is the best available proxy for a measure of official delinquency, but one should recognize its limitations. Not all arrests result in referrals to HRS. This indicator would not reflect changes in police arrest, charging, and referral practices. It does, however, provide a measure of the volume of cases HRS has had to deal with.

From table 4.2 it is clear that the overall population at risk changed very little from FY 1982–83 to FY 1988–89 (a decrease of two percent in Broward; an increase of six percent in the rest of the state). The delinquency case referrals, however, rose (35% in Broward; 58% in the rest of the state). Felony referrals were up even more sharply (56% in Broward; 63% in the rest of the state).

Tables 4.3 and 4.4 present detention admissions and ADPs, respectively, as rates based on the population at risk, the number of delinquency cases referred, and the number of felony cases referred. Each table shows the rates both for secure detention and for total detention (secure and home detention combined). Table 4.3 uses direct rather than total admissions to better reflect responses to individual cases: a single case may show up more than once in the total admissions figures, e.g., a direct admission to secure detention followed by a transfer to home detention followed by a subsequent transfer back to secure detention.

Tables 4.3 and 4.4 show that detention usage was closely related to the volume of delinquency referrals received by HRS. Interestingly, detention use appears more closely tied to overall delinquency cases than to the subset of felony cases. In other words, the seriousness of the referral charge appears to have had little effect on detention usage. The rate of secure and total detention direct admissions as a function of delinquency case referrals varied little from year to year. From FY 1982–83 to FY 1987–88, about one in three delinquency cases resulted in an admission to detention, both in Broward and the rest of the state. The change in usage of secure detention beginning in FY 1988–89 will be discussed later.

Figure 4.1 charts the rate of secure detention admissions for Broward and the rest of Florida from FY 1982–83 to FY 1990–91. It illustrates the statewide increase during the mid-80s and the extent to which Broward's rate increase was steeper. It also clearly shows the subsequent reductions that will be discussed later.

Broward Changes in Fiscal Year 1986–87

In addition to the general patterns discussed above, something appears to have happened in Broward in FY 1986–87 that resulted in an even sharper rise in detention use. Compared with FY 1985–86, direct

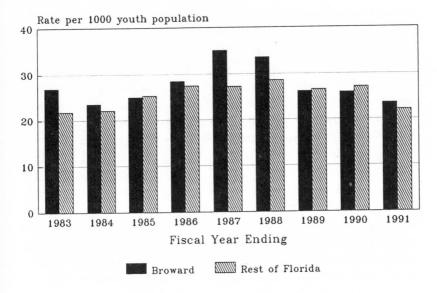

Source: HRS-CYF, Program Office

Figure 4.1. Secure detention admissions, Broward County v. rest of Florida.

admissions to secure detention increased 24% and the ADP jumped 28%, the largest single-year increases. Such increases did not occur in the rest of the state, nor did the delinquency referral volume show an unusual leap in that year. In tables 4.3 and 4.4, one can see that in FY 1986–87, Broward's rates of detention admissions and ADPs suddenly surpassed those of the rest of the state. That year did see a change in the HRS district-level administration in Broward, but no one questioned could recall any particular events or policy changes that could account for this change in detention practices. Perhaps the police took advantage of the turnover in HRS administration to bring more cases to detention.

Broward in Fiscal Year 1987–88

Although Broward's rate of direct admissions declined slightly in FY 1987–88 from FY 1986–87, the ADP increased further. As can be seen from table 4.1, the average length of stay increased between FY 1986–87 and FY 1987–88 for both secure and home detention, further boosting the ADP. By whatever measure, Broward faced an extreme crisis in detention by FY 1987–88. The secure facility, with a design capacity of

109 beds, showed an ADP of 160.9, producing an overcrowding rate of 48%. Of direct admissions to detention status, only 38 out of 3,432 (one percent) were to home detention. The volume of delinquency referrals showed no sign of abating. A lawsuit was filed against HRS seeking a reduction in its secure detention population and improvements in the conditions of detention. At that point, the Center for the Study of Youth Policy, with funding from the Casey Foundation, began its efforts to help Broward develop a constructive solution to its detention crisis.

Summary

The years 1982 to 1988 began with a system that detained a large portion of its delinquency referrals. During that period, the volume of delinquency referrals rose steeply, and the system attempted to continue its routinely high rates of detention. Secure detention facilities became overcrowded, and districts tried to adapt by transferring more cases to home detention. The strains in Broward were even more extreme, resulting in a crisis situation by 1988.

Implementation of the Broward Detention Project

Preliminary Analysis

The Project's main goal was to reduce the overcrowding of Broward's detention center. As a first step, the Center for the Study of Youth Policy conducted a preliminary analysis of the detention practices in Broward County in the Spring of 1988 to identify targets of potential intervention (Van Vleet, Butts, & Barton, 1988). After visits to the facility, interviews with several staff in HRS and other related agencies, and an analysis of the detention population, the authors concluded that HRS exercised no effective control over intake decisions, that the existing home detention program was under-utilized and held in low esteem by others in the juvenile justice community, and that other detention alternatives were nonexistent. Police and state attorneys essentially controlled intake, while the Judiciary controlled release decisions; the Judiciary also controlled some of the intake—court orders accounted for about 18% of cases securely detained, and nearly all use of home detention was by judicial transfer from secure status. HRS and public defender input was minimal. As a result, Broward appeared to detain many low-risk youths. Detention appeared to be used for "jail therapy," and the statutory length of stay guideline of 15–21 days was frequently extended by the state attorneys. More than two-thirds of the detained youths were charged with non-violent offenses, about two-thirds were black, and about one-fourth were under the age of 15.

The preliminary report concluded with several recommendations, including: the development of objective intake guidelines; increasing the involvement of the public defender's office; developing alternatives to secure detention, such as shelter care, home detention at various levels of supervision intensity, and day programming. These became the primary objectives of the Project. To implement them, the Project sought to assist with a mediated settlement of the lawsuit, strengthen the practices and perception of the existing home detention program, encourage the involvement of private providers in establishing detention alternatives, facilitate communication and cooperation among the various relevant agencies, and provide monitoring and feedback to the system through research. These efforts are described briefly below.

Mediation of the Lawsuit

As mentioned previously, one of the reasons Broward was selected as the site for the Project was the existence of a class-action lawsuit seeking population reductions and improved conditions in its detention center. Judge Orlando suggested that mediation be used to arrive at a settlement of the lawsuit. The Project identified a mediator and covered a portion of the mediation expenses. Through mediation, the parties reached a voluntary settlement calling for the gradual reduction of the detention center population to its design capacity. The settlement agreement also required that HRS cooperate with the Center for the Study of Youth Policy in the development of alternatives to secure detention.

Home Detention

The home detention program as it existed in 1988 was under-utilized. Admission to home detention occurred at the discretion of the court and almost exclusively for youths initially placed in secure detention. The program was officially called "non-secure detention" and was viewed as just that—non-secure and untrustworthy. Home detention staff, called Community Youth Leaders (CYL), were among the lowest paid HRS employees with direct case responsibility. Supervision of the youths was routine and less than intense (e.g., little or no supervision on evenings and weekends). Judges and prosecutors expressed little confidence in the program. Its performance, however, was quite good according to statewide monitoring statistics, with success rates exceeding 90% (that is, fewer than 10% committed new law violations or failed to appear for court hearings). These performance facts were not being effectively communicated.

The Project arranged for the director of the highly successful home detention program in Cuyahoga County (Cleveland), Ohio to visit Broward in December of 1988 to assess its home detention program and provide some training to its staff. The training included segments on courtroom demeanor, making behavioral supervision less predictable to youths, and more extensive accountability procedures. At the same time, a more detailed description of the home detention program, complete with different levels of supervision intensity, was drafted and circulated among the Judiciary and State Attorneys. The name of the program was changed to "home detention." The Judiciary and prosecutors began to express more confidence in home detention. Interestingly, one judge in particular began ordering many cases directly to home detention. Subsequently, the Project sent some of Broward's key detention supervisory staff to Cleveland to view firsthand some of Cuyahoga County's programs and procedures.

Daytime Report Center

In March of 1989, with financial support from the Project, the Boys Clubs of Broward began accepting some home detention youths into a day program at one of its sites. This program, whose staff included three special education teachers provided by the local school district, consisted of education, meals, and recreation. Participating youths arrived early in the morning, had basic education classes in the morning and early afternoon, and then joined the regular Boys Club after-school recreational programming. Transportation was provided by HRS, and cases remained under the supervision of a home detention worker. HRS planning discussions at the conclusion of the Project included talk of expanding this program to other Boys Club sites in the county.

Residential Alternative

The development of a residential alternative to secure detention proved to be one of the most difficult tasks faced by the Project. HRS indicated that it owned a house in a residential neighborhood that had recently been remodeled and could house six to eight youths. Representatives of several private provider agencies were invited to a meeting to discuss the possibility of operating a shelter program at that facility with the assistance of Project funds. Those attending expressed little interest in operating a detention alternative. The one agency that submitted a proposal requested a level of funding that far exceeded expectations. HRS itself drafted a proposal to run the shelter program, but at an even higher operating rate.[4]

Finally, in April of 1989, the Project threatened to withdraw its resources unless the District came up with a plan for a residential alternative to secure detention. The Lutheran Ministries of Florida, which already operated a large dependency shelter in the county, was recruited to operate a six-bed detention shelter program at the HRS-owned facility. This program opened in July of 1989.

Intake Screening

During the first year of the Project, detention intake practices remained problematic. Court-ordered assignments to secure detention rose sharply, accounting for nearly half of all secure detention admissions (formerly, 20% of secure detention admissions had been by court order). State Attorneys continued to choose secure detention at every available opportunity. From the beginning, the Project recognized the necessity of introducing an objective screening instrument that would permit HRS to prevent the secure detention of low-risk cases. However, with the control given by the statute to the court and prosecutors, such an instrument would have to meet with their approval in order to be effective.

In the summer of 1989, the Project developed a proposed Risk Assessment Instrument, modeled after those recommended by the

BROWARD JUVENILE DETENTION RISK ASSESSMENT INSTRUMENT
Revision 8: 9-6-89

Case #:_____   Name:_____   Date:_____   Screener:_____

Select the <u>highest</u> point total applicable for each category:

A. MOST SERIOUS ALLEGED CURRENT OFFENSE   _____
     12 - Murder; Attempted Murder; Manslaughter; Rape, Sexual Battery; Kidnapping;
         Armed Robbery (gun); Armed Burglary (gun); Burg. w/ Asslt./Batt.
     10 - Arson; Felony with Firearm; Aggravated Battery; Robbery w/ Weapon (exc. w/ gun);
     8 - Aggravated Assault; Concealed Firearm; Felony w/ Weapon (exc. w/ gun)
         Drug Trafficking or Manufacturing; Drug Poss. or Sale near School
     6 - Burglary (occupied dwelling); Strong-Arm Robbery; Extortion
     5 - All other Burglary (exc. burg. auto); Dealing in Stolen Property; Drug sales;
         Drug Poss. w/ intent to deliver
     4 - Burg. Auto; Stolen Vehicle; Grand Theft (Larceny over $300); Rec. Stolen Prop.;
         Drug possession; Felony Criminal Mischief; Poss. Burglary Tools
     3 - Fraud; Forgery; Resist. Arrest w/ Violence; Battery L.E.O.
     2 - Misdemeanor offenses (e.g., Simple Battery; Simple Assault; Petty Theft;
         Disorderly Conduct; Loitering and Prowling, etc.)
     1 - PUO for Technical viol. of community control, commitment program, home detention
     0 - Status Offenses (truancy, runaway, incorrigible)

B. ADDITIONAL CURRENT OFFENSES   + _____
     3 - Two or more additional current felonies
     2 - One additional current felony
     1 - One or more additional current misdemeanors

C. PRIOR OFFENSES   + _____
     5 - Two or more prior major felonies (Capital Felony; Life Felony; 1st Deg. Felony PBL;
         1st Deg. Felony; Murder-2nd or 3rd; Manslaughter; Sexual Battery; Agg. Battery)
     3 - One prior major felony (as above); Two or more other felonies
     2 - One other felony
     1 - Two or more prior misdemeanors

D. SUBTOTAL I. (Sum of A, B and C)   = _____

E. RISK OF FAILURE TO APPEAR   or _____
     10 - Pick-up order for escape/abscond from commitment program/detention/
         comm. control/furlough/aftercare program
     6 - Pick-up order for failure to appear
     3 - Evidence of prior failure to appear

F. SUBTOTAL II. (Enter larger of D <u>or</u> E)   _____

G. LEGAL STATUS   + _____
     2 - Commitment status
     1 - Community Control status; Home Detention status; Hearing pending

H. MITIGATING FACTORS (Can decrease total by 1 or 2 points. Specify:)   *(max. 2)* - (_____)

I. AGGRAVATING FACTORS (Specific threat to victims/witnesses: 3 points;   *(max. 3)* + (_____)
     Other factors can increase total by 1 or 2 points. Specify:)

J. TOTAL (Sum of F, G, H and I)   = _____

<u>SCORING:</u>   12 and up - Secure;   7 to 11 - Randomize;   0 to 6 - Release.

National Council on Crime and Delinquency (Baird, 1984). The Risk Assessment Instrument (RAI) assigned points to youths based upon the current charge, prior offense history, legal status, and evidence of failure to appear.[5] Total scores were used to place a youth into one of three categories—low risk (outright release); medium risk (home detention); and high risk (secure detention permitted).[6]

The Project tested a tentative version of such an instrument on the records of 74 cases screened during one week and demonstrated that the application of the RAI would help restrict initial assignments to secure detention and would result in more consistent decisions. The Project suggested that a local Detention Task Force, including representatives of the Court, State Attorney's Office, Public Defender's Office, HRS, and provider programs assume responsibility for modifying the proposed RAI prior to implementation. In October, the revised RAI was added to the existing HRS detention screening procedure *and* the State Attorney's Office agreed to employ it whenever its attorneys were contacted. The Court, while indicating its approval of the idea of the RAI and participating in its evolution, refused to let its court-ordered detention cases be screened with the RAI.

An analysis of the first three months of intake screening using the RAI indicated that it was functioning reasonably well. Both HRS intake staff and the State Attorney's Office expressed confidence in most of the decisions resulting from use of the RAI, and the proportion of screened cases being securely detained dropped while releases rose. The RAI clearly provided HRS with more control over the intake process than it had previously exercised. However, the Court's refusal to permit screening of cases arriving at the detention center with court orders limited the ability of the new RAI to further reduce the secure detention population. More than half (51%) of the assignments to secure detention between October and December of 1989 were by court order and thus not subject to RAI screening. The lack of support from the Judiciary limited the ability of the RAI to reserve secure detention for truly high-risk cases.

Public Defender's Involvement

Prior to the project, the Public Defender's Office rarely participated in detention matters. A new Chief of the Juvenile Division of the PD's Office assumed his duties shortly after the beginning of the project. He

exhibited much more interest in detention issues than had his predecessor. Through the efforts of the Project's attorney-liaison, the PD's
office received additional training on the state's detention statute, was
regularly informed about the Project, had some barriers to participation overcome (e.g., the PD now receives case paperwork from HRS in
a timely fashion), and filed several appellate proceedings to challenge
questionable judicial practices and orders adversely affecting detention.

Empirical Feedback

From its continuous data collection activities, the Project periodically produced reports summarizing aspects of detention practices.
These reports were directed to HRS, both at the district and state
levels, and to the other relevant agencies. A baseline report in early
1989 portrayed the continued overuse of secure detention and the
specific need for the alternative programs. Other reports in the spring
and summer of 1989 focused on the intake process, documenting the
relative lack of HRS control in comparison with that of the Court and
the State Attorney's Office. Later reports discussed the development
and monitored the implementation of the Risk Assessment Instrument
as described above. These reports helped to sustain a focus on specific
issues warranting the attention of HRS and other actors. Although not
always greeted with great enthusiasm, they helped guide ongoing
decisions.

Facilitating Communication

At the beginning of the Project, it was apparent that the various
agencies concerned with juvenile justice in Broward had developed an
informal pattern of relationships that protected the power of the Court
and prosecutors. HRS was perceived, with partial justification, as
weak and ineffective. The Public Defender was not active in detention
matters, and no other advocacy groups challenged the law-and-order
interests. The detention overcrowding situation was handled in a purely
reactive, crisis-management fashion. HRS representatives would appeal to the Court for temporary assistance in releasing some youths
from detention to ease overcrowding. Any such assistance would be
considered a favor, not the enactment of a more reasonable policy. The
judiciary, upset with the relative lack of delinquency programs in the

area, would commit and detain large numbers of youths to get the attention of HRS and force the agency to do something with these youths.[7] HRS was relatively demoralized, rarely challenged the police, Court, or prosecutors, and in fact often made its own detention intake decisions match what they knew the others would prefer. Many in HRS welcomed the detention lawsuit as a mechanism for effecting changes that they wanted to make but were unable or unwilling to initiate on their own.

The Project focused its initial efforts on HRS in an attempt to document the extent of the detention problem and to develop potential solutions. A Project Team emerged, consisting of staff from the Center for the Study of Youth Policy, District 10 HRS, and state-level HRS staff. In the Fall of 1988, the Project contracted with a local legal firm to provide consultation. One of its attorneys evolved into the primary liaison for the Project with the Court and prosecutors. She had formerly served as a State Attorney and had a good relationship with the judges and prosecutors. She effectively communicated the Project's intentions and activities to these agencies. She presented them with written descriptions of the restructured home detention program, provided training to HRS intake workers, prosecutors, and public defenders on aspects of the law relating to detention as well as on new procedures (such as the Risk Assessment Instrument) developed by the Project, solicited increased involvement from the Public Defender's Office, and informally mediated disagreements as they arose among the various agencies. Her role clearly was pivotal in promoting the Project's goals.

While the Project's attorney was the informal center of the communications network, the formal mechanism was a Task Force, mentioned above in connection with the Risk Assessment Instrument. Beginning in the spring of 1989, this group met sporadically for a year. The Task Force was intended to be a vehicle for dissemination of the Project's achievements, inter-agency communication, timely problem solving, and potential long-range, local oversight of detention issues that would sustain the Project's efforts after its conclusion. The primary accomplishment of the Task Force was the refinement and implementation of the Risk Assessment Instrument. The belated formation, irregularity of the meetings, lack of full attendance, and, perhaps, omission of certain key actors (e.g., one of the two Juvenile Court Judges) limited the effectiveness of the Task Force.

Results

The results of the Broward Detention Project indicate that Broward substantially reduced its use of secure detention while correspondingly increasing the use of home detention and other alternatives without experiencing an increase in failures to appear or subsequent offending by youths on detention status.

Changes in Detention Usage

We compared the patterns of detention usage in FY 1987–88, the last pre-project year, with those in FY 1988–89, the first year after the introduction of the project, to determine if there had been any changes in detention practices associated with the implementation of the Project. The main results are summarized in table 4.5 and suggest that:

1. Direct admissions to secure detention in Broward declined sharply in the year following the introduction of the Project.
2. The average daily population (ADP) in secure detention showed a similar decline.
3. Direct admissions to home detention increased dramatically.
4. The home detention ADP rose to match the decline in the secure detention ADP.
5. The changes in Broward detention usage were much more extreme than those in the rest of the state.
6. The changes do not appear to reflect changes in the volume of delinquency cases referred to HRS in Broward.

More specifically, there were 734 fewer direct admissions to secure detention in FY 1988–89 than in FY 1987–88, a drop of 22%. Conversely, there were 706 more direct admissions to home detention, a staggering increase considering that there had never been more than a handful of direct admissions to home detention in the past. The more traditional use of home detention, as a court-ordered change from secure status, continued at nearly the same level, so the new direct admissions created a substantial overall increase in the home detention caseloads. Figure 4.2 illustrates the changes in direct admissions to secure and home detention.

The average daily population in secure detention fell from 161 to 132,

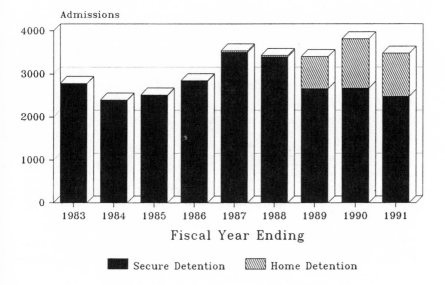

Source: HRS–CYF, Program Office

Figure 4.2. Direct detention admissions, secure and home detention, Broward County.

a decline of 18%. Although an ADP of 132 reflects continued overcrowding in a facility designed for 109 beds, the one-year reduction is still impressive. The home detention ADP rose by 42%, from 76.8 to 108.7, essentially matching the secure detention decrease. Clearly, Broward continued to place the same number of youths on detention status in FY 1988–89, but greater utilization of home detention permitted a reduction in reliance upon secure detention. Figure 4.3 illustrates the ADP changes.

Effects of the Changes

Regarding home detention outcomes, 95% of youths admitted to home detention were *not* charged with new law violations while on home detention status, and this rate did not change as a result of the increased utilization of home detention. Moreover, the rate of youths returned for new law violations in the rest of the state was virtually identical—about four percent for each of the three years. Although the number of such cases rose steadily, from 33 in FY 1987–88 to 54 in FY 1988–89 to an estimated 81 in FY 1989–90, the home detention caseload

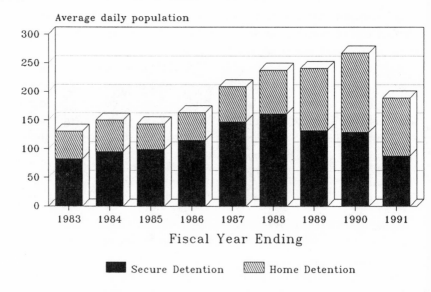

Source: HRS-CYF, Program Office

Figure 4.3. Average daily population, secure and home detention, Broward County.

rose just as steeply. When the number of cases returned for new violations is shown as a percentage of all home detention admissions, the
rate is nearly constant (four percent in FY 1987–88; four percent in FY
1988–89; five percent in FY 1989–90).

Reliable data regarding the other important indicator of home detention program performance, the rate of cases failing to appear for
court hearings, were simply not available for all of the time periods of
interest. Where data were available, for parts of FY 1989–90, the overall
FTA rate appears to have been about six percent, not indicative of a
major problem in absolute terms. Stated otherwise, even after the Project's interventions, 94% of home detention cases *did* appear in court.

Costs

The operating cost of secure detention averaged $50 per day per
youth in FY 1987–88, while home detention's per diem was about $10.
The Boys Club day program and shelter per diems were about $14 and
$85, respectively. In a report discussing refinancing options for Brow-
ard's juvenile justice system, the Center for the Study of Social Policy

(1990) showed that the additional costs of the alternatives and increased use of home detention were more than matched by savings from the reduced use of secure detention.

Furthermore, Broward was able to avoid the cost of building additional detention capacity. Had the detention center remained as overcrowded as it was in 1988, Broward might have needed to build an additional 50 to 60 beds. Construction costs for such a facility were estimated at $2.5 to $3 million, along with operating costs of about $1 million per year (CSSP, 1990).

Continued Overcrowding

Although the Project certainly helped produce a reduction in the use of secure detention in Broward, the detention center remained overcrowded at the conclusion of the project in June of 1990. Despite analyses that consistently revealed a large number of relatively low risk cases among the detainees (even after the changes in practices noted above) and despite the introduction of the Risk Assessment Instrument designed to prevent such detentions, the population remained an average of 21% beyond capacity. This continued overcrowding appeared to be due to three primary factors: an increase in court-ordered secure detention; an increase in the use of secure detention for committed cases awaiting placement, and an average length of stay (LOS) that exceeded the statewide average by more than two days.

In terms of absolute numbers, court orders for secure detention increased from an average of 45 per month in the fall of 1988 to 102 per month in the fall of 1989, even after the introduction of the Risk Assessment Instrument. In FY 1988–89, there were an average of 21 committed youths awaiting placement in the Broward detention center, or about 16% of the secure detention population on any given day. In FY 1989–90, there were 32 such youths detained on a given day, or nearly one-fourth (23.7%) of the secure detention population. Nearly two-thirds of these were detained beyond the five-day statutory limit. Finally, although an average LOS difference of between two and three days may not seem like much, it can have a sizable effect on the average daily population. For example, given the FY 1988–89 rate of total admissions to secure detention in Broward, a reduction in the average LOS from 16.6 to the statewide average of 14.0 would have reduced the average daily population in secure detention by 20, from 132 to 112.

Summary

Broward made major changes in its detention practices between 1987 and 1990, reducing the use of secure detention by increasing the use of home detention and other alternatives. These changes were not accompanied by any increased risk to public safety. Moreover, the changes did not involve increased costs to the system, and may have saved the county the major expense of building additional detention bed capacity. To this extent, the project was clearly successful. The inability of the Project to enlist judicial cooperation or to affect length of stay, however, prevented the immediate achievement of even greater changes in Broward's detention practices.

Aftermath

The Broward story does not end with the official termination of the project in June of 1990. As seen in table 4.1, Broward's secure detention average daily population for FY 1990–91 had fallen to 88, well below capacity. For the month of July, 1991, it stood at 55. Admissions to secure detention continued to decline, despite continued increases in the volume of delinquency cases. Moreover, the average length of stay in Broward's secure detention center dropped from 16 days in FY 1989–90 (2 days above that of the rest of the state) to 11.9 in FY 1990–91 (2 days below the rest of the state). Finally, in FY 1990–91, the rest of Florida showed a sharp decrease in direct admissions to secure detention (a 17% reduction) and in the ADP (a 14% drop). As described below, three key events occurring shortly afterward helped consolidate and further the gains begun by the project.

In its 1990 session, the Florida legislature enacted a major juvenile justice reform package. In his capacity as chair of a statewide juvenile justice task force, Judge Orlando was instrumental in getting many of the changes in detention policies and practices begun in Broward County included in that legislation. For example, the legislation redefined the role of the relevant agencies in making detention intake decisions, in effect reducing the power of the prosecutors and increasing the authority of HRS intake workers. It also mandated the statewide use of an objective intake screening instrument modeled after the one piloted in Broward. Finally, it mandated the use of non-secure detention alternatives in all districts.

Significantly, at the end of 1990, the Juvenile Court judges in Broward rotated off the bench. The incoming judges were highly supportive of the detention reform policies and cooperated well with HRS in limiting intake to secure detention. With less opposition from other agencies than in previous years, Carl Sanniti (the HRS District Chief of Delinquency Services) was better able to monitor intake, maintain the non-secure alternatives, and institute procedures for limiting length of stay in detention.

In conclusion, Broward County has drastically reduced its use of secure juvenile detention and has paved the way for similar changes in the rest of the state. The experience of the detention project, bolstered by the subsequent legislative changes and an improved local political climate, was instrumental in bringing about this reduction. Of course, as discussed in more detail in chapter 7, such gains can be fragile. One lesson from Florida's 1980 detention reform attempt was that legislation can be reversed quickly. Further turnover on the Juvenile Court bench, changes in the local HRS administration, or a few well-publicized incidents of home detention or released youths committing serious crimes pending their court hearings could jeopardize the reforms. Much will depend upon the continued local efforts of those supporting the reforms in anticipating and countering future threats to the gains.

Appendix: Tables

Table 4.1
Detention Admissions, Average Daily Population, and Length of Stay, by Year, Broward v. Rest of Florida

	Total Admissions	Direct Admissions	ADP	LOS
		Secure Detention		
1982–83				
Broward	2,895	2,781	82.7	10.4
Rest of Florida	26,313	23,028	933.6	12.7
1983–84				
Broward	2,498	2,390	95.1	13.9
Rest of Florida	26,626	23,394	938.3	13.0
1984–85				
Broward	2,611	2,501	99.1	13.9
Rest of Florida	30,107	26,800	1,077.8	13.2
1985–86				
Broward	2,973	2,838	114.9	14.1
Rest of Florida	32,967	29,409	1,201.9	13.4
1986–87				
Broward	3,644	3,505	147.2	14.7
Rest of Florida	33,412	29,551	1,278.0	14.0
1987–88				
Broward	3,649	3,394	160.9	16.1
Rest of Florida	37,192	31,474	1,399.6	14.0
1988–89				
Broward	2,909	2,660	132.0	16.6
Rest of Florida	37,356	29,627	1,412.0	14.0
1989–90				
Broward	2,938	2,673	129.1	16.0
Rest of Florida	38,828	30,722	1,500.7	14.1
1990–91				
Broward	2,700	2,484	88.0	11.9
Rest of Florida	31,663	25,753	1,285.9	14.8
		Home Detention		
1982–83				
Broward	436	4	47.8	40.0
Rest of Florida	5,746	358	316.8	21.5
1983–84				
Broward	338	9	54.6	59.1
Rest of Florida	5,938	287	339.9	23.0
1984–85				
Broward	509	13	44.1	31.7
Rest of Florida	6,637	330	413.9	23.5

	Total Admissions	Direct Admissions	ADP	LOS
1985–86				
Broward	545	12	48.0	32.1
Rest of Florida	7,675	364	469.0	23.0
1986–87				
Broward	867	35	61.8	26.0
Rest of Florida	8,605	531	544.8	23.4
1987–88				
Broward	854	38	76.8	32.9
Rest of Florida	11,197	763	693.3	23.4
1988–89				
Broward	1,515	744	108.7	26.2
Rest of Florida	12,184	1,630	773.2	23.5
1989–90				
Broward	2,158	1,145	138.5	23.4
Rest of Florida	12,735	2,072	943.4	27.0
1990–91				
Broward	2,174	997	100.7	16.9
Rest of Florida	11,983	2,559	993.2	30.3

Source: HRS-CYF Program Office.

Note: ADP=average daily population; LOS=average length of stay.

Table 4.2

Juvenile Population, Delinquency Cases Referred to HRS and Felony Cases Referred to HRS by Year, Broward v. Rest of Florida

	Pop. at Risk (10–17 yrs.)	Delinquency Cases	Rate per 1,000 Pop.	Felony Cases	Rate per 1,000 Pop.
1982–83					
Broward	103,470	7,611	73.6	2,991	28.9
Rest of Florida	1,054,735	65,091	61.7	27,326	25.9
1983–84					
Broward	101,669	7,419	73.0	2,968	29.2
Rest of Florida	1,057,178	65,929	62.4	27,178	25.7
1984–85					
Broward	100,060	8,436	84.3	3,130	31.3
Rest of Florida	1,059,754	72,251	68.2	30,113	28.4
1985–86					
Broward	99,808	8,535	85.8	3,713	37.2
Rest of Florida	1,073,040	79,286	73.9	34,138	31.8
1986–87					
Broward	99,869	9,628	96.4	3,919	39.2
Rest of Florida	1,085,362	88,767	81.8	35,734	32.9

continued

Table 4.2

Juvenile Population, Delinquency Cases Referred to HRS and Felony Cases Referred to HRS by Year, Broward v. Rest of Florida *continued*

	Pop. at Risk (10–17 yrs.)	Delinquency Cases	Rate per 1,000 Pop.	Felony Cases	Rate per 1,000 Pop.
1987–88					
Broward	100,952	9,937	98.4	4,213	41.7
Rest of Florida	1,098,293	97,004	88.3	40,702	37.1
1988–89					
Broward	101,728	10,290	101.1	4,651	45.7
Rest of Florida	1,118,172	103,155	92.3	44,471	39.8
1989–90					
Broward	103,382	10,639	102.9	4,543	43.9
Rest of Florida	1,135,703	109,076	96.0	46,815	41.2
1990–91					
Broward	105,708	11,488	108.7	4,940	46.7
Rest of Florida	1,167,854	115,787	99.1	47,879	41.0

Source: HRS-CYF Program Office.

Table 4.3

Secure Detention and Total Detention Direct Admission Rates Per Population at Risk, Delinquency Cases, and Felony Cases, by Year, Broward v. Rest of Florida

	Secure Detention Admissions			Total Detention Admissions*		
	Rate per 1,000 Population	Rate per 100 Delinquency Cases	Rate per 100 Felony Cases	Rate per 1,000 Population	Rate per 100 Delinquency Cases	Rate per 100 Felony Cases
1982–83						
Broward	26.9	36.5	93.0	26.9	36.6	93.1
Rest of Florida	21.8	35.4	84.3	22.2	35.9	85.6
1983–84						
Broward	23.5	32.2	80.5	23.6	32.3	80.8
Rest of Florida	22.1	35.5	86.1	22.4	35.9	87.1
1984–85						
Broward	25.0	29.6	79.9	25.1	29.8	80.3
Rest of Florida	25.3	37.1	89.0	25.6	37.5	90.1
1985–86						
Broward	28.4	33.3	76.4	28.6	33.4	76.8
Rest of Florida	27.4	37.1	86.1	27.7	37.6	87.2
1986–87						
Broward	35.1	36.4	89.4	35.4	36.8	90.3
Rest of Florida	27.2	33.3	82.7	27.7	33.9	84.2

	Secure Detention Admissions			Total Detention Admissions*		
	Rate per 1,000 Population	Rate per 100 Delinquency Cases	Rate per 100 Felony Cases	Rate per 1,000 Population	Rate per 100 Delinquency Cases	Rate per 100 Felony Cases
1987–88						
Broward	33.6	34.2	80.6	34.0	34.5	81.5
Rest of Florida	28.6	32.4	77.3	29.4	33.2	79.2
1988–89						
Broward	26.1	25.9	57.2	33.5	33.1	73.2
Rest of Florida	26.5	28.7	66.6	28.0	30.3	70.3
1989–90						
Broward	25.9	25.1	58.8	36.9	35.9	84.0
Rest of Florida	27.1	28.2	65.6	28.9	30.1	70.1
1990–91						
Broward	23.5	21.6	50.3	32.9	30.3	70.5
Rest of Florida	22.1	22.2	53.8	24.2	24.5	59.1

Source: HRS-CYF Program Office.
*Total detention includes both secure and home detention.

Table 4.4
Secure Detention and Total Detention Average Daily Population Rates
Per Population at Risk, Delinquency Cases, and Felony Cases, by Year,
Broward v. Rest of Florida

	Secure Detention ADP			Total Detention ADP*		
	Rate per 100K Population	Rate per 1,000 Delinquency Cases	Rate per 1,000 Felony Cases	Rate per 100K Population	Rate per 1,000 Delinquency Cases	Rate per 1,000 Felony Cases
1982–83						
Broward	79.9	10.9	27.6	126.1	17.1	43.6
Rest of Florida	88.5	14.3	34.2	117.6	19.1	45.4
1983–84						
Broward	93.5	12.8	32.0	147.2	20.2	50.4
Rest of Florida	88.8	14.2	34.5	120.9	19.4	47.0
1984–85						
Broward	99.0	11.7	31.7	143.1	17.0	45.8
Rest of Florida	101.7	14.9	35.8	140.8	20.6	49.5
1985–86						
Broward	115.1	13.5	30.9	163.2	19.1	43.9
Rest of Florida	112.0	15.2	35.2	155.7	21.1	48.9

continued

Table 4.4

Secure Detention and Total Detention Average Daily Population Rates
Per Population at Risk, Delinquency Cases, and Felony Cases, by Year,
Broward v. Rest of Florida *continued*

	Secure Detention ADP			Total Detention ADP*		
	Rate per 100K Population	Rate per 1,000 Delinquency Cases	Rate per 1,000 Felony Cases	Rate per 100K Population	Rate per 1,000 Delinquency Cases	Rate pe 1,000 Felony Cases
1986–87						
Broward	147.4	15.3	37.6	209.3	21.7	53.3
Rest of Florida	117.7	14.4	35.8	167.9	20.5	51.0
1987–88						
Broward	159.4	16.2	38.2	235.5	23.9	56.4
Rest of Florida	127.4	14.4	34.4	190.6	21.6	51.4
1988–89						
Broward	129.8	12.8	28.4	236.6	23.4	51.8
Rest of Florida	126.3	13.7	31.8	195.4	21.2	49.1
1989–90						
Broward	124.9	12.1	28.4	258.8	25.1	58.9
Rest of Florida	132.1	13.8	32.1	215.2	22.4	52.2
1990–91						
Broward	83.2	7.7	17.8	178.5	16.4	38.2
Rest of Florida	110.1	11.1	26.9	195.1	19.7	47.6

Source: HRS-CYF Program Office.

*Total detention includes both secure and home detention.

Table 4.5

Summary of Changes From FY 87–88 to FY 88–89, Broward v. Rest of Florida

		FY 87–88	FY 88–89	Change (%)
Admissions, Secure:	Broward	3,394	2,660	−22
	Rest of Florida	31,474	29,627	−06
Avg. Daily Pop., Secure:	Broward	160.9	132.0	−18
	Rest of Florida	1,399.6	1,412.0	+01
Admissions, Home Det.:	Broward	38	744	+1858
	Rest of Florida	763	1,630	+114
Transfers in, Home Det.:	Broward	816	771	−06
	Rest of Florida	10,434	11,554	+11
Avg. Daily Pop., Home Det.:	Broward	76.8	108.7	+42
	Rest of Florida	693.3	773.2	+12
Delinquency Cases Rec'd:	Broward	9,937	10,290	+04
	Rest of Florida	97,004	103,155	+06
Felony Cases Rec'd:	Broward	4,213	4,651	+10
	Rest of Florida	40,702	44,471	+09

Source: HRS-CYF Program Office.

Notes

Portions of this chapter have been adapted from William H. Barton, "Promoting Change in Juvenile Detention: The Broward County Experience," paper presented at the annual meetings of the American Society of Criminology, Baltimore, November, 1990, and from Barton, "The Broward Juvenile Detention Project: A Case Study in Implementation," unpublished report, Center for the Study of Youth Policy, University of Michigan, June 1990. Others who provided information for parts of this chapter include Christina Spudeas, Leonard Matarese, Kim Gorsuch, and Deborah Willis of the Center for the Study of Youth Policy. Special thanks are due to Steve Ray, Program Office, HRS Department of Children, Youth and Families, who made available much of the aggregate data used in this report. HRS District 10 administrators and staff at the Broward Detention Center, especially Michelle Parrish, Yvonne Presley, Cassandra Wright, Ron Fryer, Jerry Wescott, and Carl Sanniti, also helped provide data. The Project also benefited from the interested involvement of an Advisory Panel that consisted of C. Ronald Huff, Larry LeFlore, Paul Lerman, Charles Massey, and Robert Schwartz. The authors, however, assume complete responsibility for the conclusions and opinions expressed in this chapter.

1. State Attorneys were also to be contacted even in some instances of police-intake *agreement* (e.g., if they agreed to recommend release for cases charged with certain offenses).

2. Florida's fiscal year runs from July 1 to June 30.

3. A reminder about that rate appears in order. Recall that Florida had one of the highest rates of detention in the nation during the 1980s, exceeded by only three states, according to a 1987 national survey.

4. The HRS District administration showed other signs of being less than fully committed to establishing an alternative detention shelter, including raising a concern that local zoning regulations might prevent the use of their building as a detention alternative. Upon investigation by the Project, this concern proved unfounded. The HRS District administration apparently preferred to reserve the facility for use as a shelter for dependent children rather than as a detention alternative.

5. A copy of the instrument as eventually implemented is appended to this paper.

6. The Florida statute did not specify *mandatory* secure detention under any circumstances; rather, it specified that secure detention was *not* to be used under certain conditions and could only be *considered* if certain other conditions were met. In actual practice, however, we assumed that all or most of the high-scoring, "high-risk" youths would be securely detained.

7. In May of 1987, the settlement of a statewide lawsuit, known as *Bobby M.*, resulted in the reduction of training school beds and the (supposed) substitution of a "continuum" of community-based alternatives. Delays in implement-

ing the alternatives, along with the reduced institutional capacity, angered many judges and prosecutors in the state who would prefer to commit more youths to residential placements.

Bibliography

Baird, S. C. (1984). *Classification of juveniles in corrections*. Madison, WI: National Council on Crime and Delinquency.

Center for the Study of Social Policy (CSSP). (1990). *Refinancing Broward County's juvenile justice system*. Washington, D.C.: Center for the Study of Social Policy.

Florida Department of Health and Rehabilitative Services (HRS). (1981). *A report on the impact of detention-related changes made in the Juvenile Justice Act in 1980*. Tallahassee: HRS, Office of Evaluation and Children, Youth and Families Program Office.

McNeese, C. A., & Ezell, M. (1983). Political symbolism in juvenile justice—Reforming Florida's juvenile detention criteria. *Journal of Sociology and Social Welfare, 10,* 242–58.

Orlando, F. A., & Barton, W. H. (1989). *The juvenile detention crisis in Florida*. Ann Arbor, MI: Center for the Study of Youth Policy.

Van Vleet, R. K., Butts, J. A., & Barton, W. H. (1988). *An analysis of the Broward County Juvenile Detention Center*. Ann Arbor, MI: Center for the Study of Youth Policy.

5

Controlling Juvenile Detention Population: Strategies for Reform

CARL V. SANNITI

This chapter will illustrate how a detention center population can be controlled through development of detention admission criteria, screening instruments, and careful monitoring and expediting of children in detention. It is important to realize that the number of children at risk and even the number of official complaints has little bearing on the number of admissions, and that even a small reduction in average length of stay can have significant impact on the detention population.

Detention centers have changed. You must understand that. Fifteen years ago, the principal concerns of a detention center superintendent were safety and security. While those are still concerns today, many detention centers also run large home detention programs and shelter facilities. Superintendents are now concerned about appropriateness of alternative education programs, self-directed computer instruction programs, low fat diets, mental health screening, and upgrading medical and dental services inside the facility. Today a superintendent is a business manager and treatment specialist as well as a jailer.

With an increase in the number of lawsuits brought against overcrowded facilities, and a growing public concern about quality of life within our facilities, population control has become a major issue. But population control is difficult, and many superintendents feel a great deal of frustration at being held responsible for something over which they feel they have no control. Population can be controlled, and I hope to be able to illustrate that the principal ingredient needed is a *firm* commitment from the top administrator to each detention intake screener and home detention worker that this is an organizational priority.

"Detention" Has Changed

Over the past 15 years, detention centers have changed from holding facilities most people would like to ignore into places of true excitement. Many new and innovative things are happening in detention, both inside and outside the facilities. The superintendent's role has changed dramatically in both Cuyahoga and Broward counties; we have begun selecting assistant superintendents with specific experience and skills in order to address the multiple program needs at these facilities. Both facilities, over a thousand miles away from each other and in very different organizational structures, have found it necessary to assign one assistant superintendent to intake, population control, home detention, and shelter care; one to the secure area; and another individual to administrative duties.

Not only have detention centers changed, but both the concept and even the definition of "detention" have changed. Today the term detention refers to a continuum of more restrictive care. Secure detention is the final alternative, to be used when less restrictive alternatives have proven unsuccessful or would endanger the safety of the community. It is this changing definition and the emergence of this new concept of detention as a continuum that give facility managers the opportunity to control their populations.

The Building of the Continuum

Essential to any attempt to control population is putting into effect necessary policy changes as well as developing alternative programs. There are four basic requirements to any population control program.

Administrative Commitment

Locking people up is easy, popular, and safe. Conversely, it is not always popular for intake staff to say no or insist on alternative placements to police officers, judges, prosecutors, and often parents, who feel secure detention is the only acceptable placement. Current research, as well as my own experience, has shown that appropriate alternative placement programs do not endanger public safety, and in view of jail overcrowding, the alternative may be the "safe" placement.

Therefore, a firm commitment from the administrative judge or top administrator to back up their intake staff's decisions for alternative placement is crucial.

Intake Policies and Guidelines

There must be written guidelines that clearly outline the detention admission criteria. A clear, concise policy is essential. Judges, intake, probation, and police officers must be aware of which children are appropriate for detention services. Such policy will also serve as a reference guide and decision-making tool for intake staff, as well as provide an instrument for supervisors or the facility administrator to use to measure their intake staff's adherence to policy. Remember, it is very easy to admit someone, especially at 2:00 A.M. with an enraged police officer or parent demanding that you do so.

Risk Screening Instrument

A policy is not enough. It is too subjective; personalities can begin to dictate its effectiveness. While policy should outline eligibility for detention status, once it has been established that an individual meets the requirements for detention status, a well-designed screening instrument should be employed to determine the appropriate detention service. This format "institutionalizes" the population control program and prevents its success from being dependent on an administrator's personal objectives.

Population control programs tend to be personality based. It seems that when the top administrator or judge feels that population control is an organizational priority, population goes down; if the administrator or judge changes and population control is no longer an organizational priority, population will increase. All of us to some extent work in our own self interest, and it is certainly easier for intake staff to hold someone else accountable rather than be held accountable if a released youth subsequently commits an offense. The judge will be sure the staff member appears at the next hearing. Home detention and shelter program managers can get rid of difficult cases and instill "credibility" in their programs. Holding someone who meets detention policy criteria is a safe, easy decision. A screening instrument used on all individuals who meet detention criteria guards against this and provides for a greater degree of accountability in decision-making.

Facility Expeditor

A Facility Expeditor is necessary in order to ensure that the cases of youths in detention are prepared and docketed for court as quickly as possible.

There are two ways to control a detention center's population: reduce admissions and reduce average length of stay. Reducing either will have an impact on your population, but reducing your average length of stay is easy and free: no program start-up cost, no difficult screening instrument to develop, no training staff, not even any philosophical arguments about who should or should not be held.

Expediting the population is simply good management. It has nothing to do with the argument of who should or should not be held, since they are already held. Moreover, detention centers are not treatment facilities, so whether or not the individual is going to be released or committed does not matter; it is simply good management to get the case to disposition as soon as possible. The fact that expediting the population will have a significant impact on a center's population is another strong argument for this non-philosophical management practice. As an example of how significant reducing average length of stay can be, in the State of Florida in 1988–89, the Leon County Detention Center had 1,472 admissions, while a similar facility in Marion County had 961 admissions (see table 5.1). But while Leon County had an average length of stay (ALS) of 6.5 days and an average daily population of 26.1, Marion County had an ALS of 19.3 and a daily average population of 50.7. The Marion facility therefore provided almost 9,000 more days of care than did Leon, even though Marion had 511 fewer admissions. Obviously the operating costs at Marion had to be greater than those at Leon; therefore, expediting your population can be viewed as an economic decision as well as a sound management practice.

The Cuyahoga County Experience

The Juvenile Court in Cleveland, Ohio, has a very favorable situation for population control, favorable because the Juvenile Court operated the detention center, clerk's office, probation, intake, and alternative services. All variables having an impact on the detention center's population were under the control of the administrative judge and court administrator. The court had progressive, experienced leadership, a home detention program, written policy and procedure on detention admission, experienced detention intake staff, and a network of shelter care beds.

Concerns and frustrations about the detention center population surfaced every six or seven months when the population rose. Supervisors and staff would have meetings and review the detention center population, and when the population returned to an acceptable level, everyone returned to their routines. Probation officers continued to return clients to the detention center for a variety of reasons, the decision based generally on the officer's personal temperament. Our shelter-care facilities would reject referrals made by the detention center referees, or refuse to accept referrals after 3:30 P.M. or on weekends. Home detention workers would return clients for contact violations at their own discretion, would reject certain referrals from the intake referees as unacceptable, and would not accept referrals after 4:30 P.M. or on weekends. Children who the intake referees felt were not appropriate for secure detention and who should be on either home detention or shelter would have to wait until the next morning or stay in detention over the weekend until the home detention and shelter staff arrived.

Everyone works in their own self-interest, and as the Home Detention Project Director, I had little concern about the detention center population. Home detention, intake, and shelter programs were not even supervised by the detention center superintendent. In fact, none of the programs having an impact on the detention center population were under the superintendent's control. All of the staff had seen enough of the court statistics to know that the number of official delinquency complaints and the population at risk had little to do with the number of admissions to the center. All of the program managers continued to manage their programs in an efficient manner to meet their program goals and objectives, which were not necessarily parallel to those of the detention center.

This fragmentation of program rationales was recognized by the court administrator, who placed all of the alternative services under one person who had authority and accountability to effect changes and to direct staff in order to manage all of the controllable variables impacting on detention population.

The following new policies and procedures were implemented:

This position, responsible for intake population management and alternative services, was placed under the superintendent of detention, hence population control was now in our self interest.

Every child held by intake was re-screened to ensure that the least restrictive alternative was utilized.

"As soon as possible" was the new time standard for conducting detention hearings; the 48-hour state law was certainly far too long.

Rather than waiting until the next morning intake admission paperwork was taken to the clerk's office immediately in order to expedite the docketing of the case.

All cases admitted at intake were tracked to ensure that the matter went to court within our targeted time frames.

We developed a daily computerized detention list with a narrative of each case describing its current status. This list could be updated daily, and each case was updated once a week.

We tracked each case placed in detention by the presiding jurist to ensure that the file left the courtroom and was returned to the assignment department.

We tracked each case placed in detention by the presiding jurist to ensure that any orders placed on the file by the judge were being carried out and in order to ensure that the case was able to go forward on the next court date.

We established a 24-hour emergency shelter-care program so that unruly juveniles (status offenders) apprehended on warrants would not have to go into detention.

We limited courtesy holds to 24 hours.

Courtesy holds from other jurisdictions no longer meant automatic hold in detention; they were instead screened as any new admission would be.

We worked closely with the court's assignment manager, reviewing the detention docket on a daily basis and advancing those cases that were ready for court to the earliest possible date.

We carefully screened requests to return children who had committed technical violations of home detention or shelter care to secure detention.

We established a procedure which allowed the release of children to home detention overnight and on weekends.

We expedited home detention and shelter care populations to ensure openings in those programs for referrals from the detention center.

These efforts were very successful, and by the end of 1989, seven and a half months later, we were able to not only reduce the detention center's population, but the decrease in the detention center population was almost exactly reflected in the increase in home detention and shelter-care programs, making them true alternatives to secure detention.

The new challenge for 1989 was crack cocaine, as it made its full presence known in Cuyahoga County. Certain policy changes were also made which required that a child brought to the detention center for the sale of cocaine be held. A new jurist on the bench brought a new philosophy and belief that a larger detention center, not fewer admissions, was the answer to population overcrowding. One might agree that an individual apprehended for dealing crack cocaine should be held at least until the matter could be reviewed by a judge, but not much time elapsed until every child apprehended with even the smallest amount of crack was initially charged with trafficking. The court's policy change may have been an appropriate response to a significant social problem, but we saw our admissions and daily average population increase. Either admissions or average length of stay had to be reduced.

New techniques were needed to respond to these new policies. We instituted the following programs in order to reduce admissions and average length of stay:

Children apprehended on warrants would go to court the same or next day.

We produced a 30-day alert form, in order to produce action on any case stuck in the system.

We instituted a warrant "scrub down." The Court had an estimated 5,000 outstanding warrants, many of which were duplicate warrants or simply no longer valid. A system was devised such that if a court hearing was held after a warrant was issued, the warrant was automatically deleted. A new warrant would not be accepted if there was already an outstanding warrant. Of course we had an override provision for new first degree felony warrants.

A staff-secure shelter-care program was developed to handle children considered too aggressive for our regular shelter program.

By the end of 1989, there was an increase in detention population, but a new equilibrium had been established. Admissions and the population had increased owing to crack cocaine and new policy changes, but new population policies and programs had been developed to meet those challenges.

The equilibrium was apparently disrupted in January 1990 with the change in administrative judges and the resignations of the court administrator and the manager of alternatives, the position responsible for population control. Since January 1, 1990, the detention center has seen a significant increase in the number of admissions, as well as average length of stay (see table 5.2 and chapter 2 in this volume). The court is a progressive, well-managed agency that will certainly resolve this problem.

The Broward Experience

The Broward Regional Juvenile Detention Center (BRJDC) is currently under a federal court order to reduce population and to improve quality of life. The Center for the Study of Youth Policy (CSYP), brought in to mediate the lawsuit, made several significant changes at the BRJDC. CSYP established detention criteria, using a detention-screening instrument with the outcome dictating what, if any, level of detention (secure, home, or shelter care) the youth would require. CSYP developed a shelter care facility and upgraded the home detention program to a credible alternative to secure care. Most important, the judges, state's attorney, police, and the plaintiff's attorney agreed to this screening instrument.

While the CSYP had made significant progress, the population of the center was still too high to settle the lawsuit. When the CSYP staff, during their monitoring, reported several incidents where screening was done "improperly" and children were held who should have been released, the superintendent and administrator intensified efforts to reduce population by reducing admissions and the length of stay. The following procedures were instituted to meet those goals:

Clear understanding throughout the delinquency system that, within reason, reducing the detention center population was a principal organizational goal that staff were expected to support and work toward.

The superintendent of detention is responsible for population control, and staff are expected to cooperate with and support his efforts.
Development of a second screening process. All children detained at intake are reviewed by the assistant superintendent.
Development of a facility expediter position. This person reviews and expedites all cases in the BRJDC. Children who appear suitable for release are placed on the docket for Superintendent Review.
A new urgency was assigned to tasks given from the detention review committee in order to expedite cases and assign them very short completion dates.
Development of good communication avenues with the judges, state's attorney, and public defenders.

Since instituting these procedures, the detention center staff has been able to reduce the daily average population to 111.6 and the length of stay to 11.3. In October 1990, our average daily population was 92, the lowest it had been since 1985. While a great deal of the superintendent's time is spent on population control, the population size no longer affects our every decision. We are able to address quality of life issues and prepare for our re-accreditation (see table 5.3).

The Critical Element to Controlled Population

No step-by-step blueprint will eliminate overcrowding. Martin's report (1989) tracking population trends of the Cuyahoga County Juvenile Court over the last 30 years and population trends for the last three and a half years in Broward County, Florida—a totally different system—point to one common factor. Whenever reducing a detention center's population becomes an organizational priority, population goes down. When administration changes, population tends to increase. Martin's report clearly confirms that both number of delinquent complaints and size of the population at risk have little to do with the number of admissions to a center. While detention criteria and risk classification instruments are essential, their use must be constantly monitored. If the agency is not committed to controlling population, the detention center's population will increase and will eventually influence every decision the agency makes.

Appendix: Tables

Table 5.1
Secure Detention Populations in Two Florida Detention Centers,
1 July 1988–30 June 1989

Facility	No. of Admissions	Resident Days	ALS (days)	ADP
Leon	1,472	9,510	6.5	26.1
Marion	961	18,505	19.3	50.7

Source: Florida Department of HRS.

Table 5.2
Cuyahoga County Juvenile Detention Center Population

	1990	1989	1988	1987
	Average Daily Population			
January	119.7	82.4	99.1	105.2
February	136.2	85.9	116.9	122.9
March	117.1	94.3	107.0	106.4
April	124.8	121.6	122.6	100.0
May	144.6	117.8	86.0	103.2
June	150.3	103.9	84.4	108.9
July	144.8	107.0	79.3	107.5
August	136.4	123.7	74.8	87.0
September	124.6	118.5	74.4	86.0
October	152.8	116.6	84.1	90.2
November	167.0	131.7	84.3	88.5
December	146.8	112.8	76.5	95.5
Year to Date	138.7	109.8	90.7	99.9
	Average Length of Stay (days)			
January	13.5	13.4	11.0	15.4
February	13.5	10.3	13.0	15.1
March	13.2	10.3	12.2	15.8
April	12.7	11.0	12.0	15.0
May	12.6	11.7	12.2	14.6
June	12.7	15.7	12.2	14.4
July	13.3	15.6	12.0	14.4
August	13.4	15.7	11.8	14.6
September	13.8	15.8	11.7	14.0
October	13.8	16.0	11.5	14.7

	1990	1989	1988	1987
November	14.4	15.7	11.5	14.3
December	14.4	12.3	12.0	12.2
Year to Date	13.4	12.2	12.0	13.1*
Total admissions	3,820	3,590	3,266	2,778

Source: Cuyahoga County Juvenile Detention Center.
*Average stay for 1987 includes the Home Detention Program of 14.6.

Table 5.3
Broward Regional Juvenile Detention Center Population

	No. of Admissions	Average Length of Stay (days)	Average Daily Population
1987	3,158	18.1	156.5
1988	3,000	18.3	150.6
1989	2,921	15.3	122.6
1990	2,853	13.9	108.6

Source: Florida Department of HRS.

Bibliography

Martin, T. (1989, April). *Forecasting secure detention bedspace needs of the Cuyahoga County Juvenile Court*. Beaverton, OR: Law and Policy Associates.

6

Toward a Model Secure Detention Program: Lessons from Shuman Center

JOSEPH T. CHRISTY

Even under the best circumstances, some children awaiting juvenile court hearings need to be held securely in the interest of public safety. Juvenile detention deprives children of their liberty while it assumes the crucial responsibility of their care. The impact detention has on both residents and the community creates an obligation for detention centers to operate effectively and to achieve a high level of quality.

As director of the juvenile detention center for Allegheny County in Pittsburgh, I take that obligation seriously. When I took over management of the center, I dreamed of shaping it into a place of excellence. I had a vivid image of what that meant—no abuse, no escapes, no overcrowding. It meant creating a setting where residents felt safe and could learn and grow. It also meant what at first seems a contradiction: designing a setting that is both secure and open to the community. Foremost, it meant developing a skilled, caring, confident staff.

Voices around me kept telling me what was *not* possible. About residents they said: "We don't have them long enough to make a difference." About the community the message was: "Let the public in and they'll just look for what's wrong." About staff I was told: "They aren't really committed to working with kids." After listening to what could not be done, I set out to do it anyway—by surrounding myself with people who believed differently from the nay-sayers. I knew organizational change was a long and arduous endeavor, but I never doubted the possibility. I also knew the key was leadership, leadership by a core group in critical positions who held in common the vision of excellence. Over the years, reality gradually came to resemble the vision. The remaking of the organization is still a work in progress and probably always will be. But it is under way.

The elements required to reshape juvenile detention are not unlike the principles that underlie change in any organization. They include the tangible work of organizational analysis, policy-making, staff selection and training, and program development as well as the less tangible qualities of leadership and commitment. Those responsible for juvenile detention need to do the hard work of managing day-to-day operations and at the same time keep their eyes fixed on the broader vision. The risk of pursuing a vision is that obstacles to achieving it and temporary shortfalls can undermine faith in it. In the midst of challenges, managers need to be steadfast. The capacity to keep the vision over time and through adversity is the hallmark of character and of leadership.

Without losing sight of these less tangible elements, it is important to identify the concrete steps required to build a successful program. Although detention centers are complex organizations that vary in size and structure, the elements that make for an optimum model are universal. Certain policies and practices promote success whether a center serves 10 or 100 clients on a given day. The same policies and practices can work in state, county, or regional systems and in both private and public operations. Regardless of size and structure, effective performance depends on understanding the external environment in which detention operates and on clarity about the mission or purpose of detention.

The external environment of detention is uncertain and changing. Demographics, economic conditions, law enforcement policies, and public mood affect detention trends. In addition, detention interacts by necessity with a network of individuals and agencies: police, courts, probation officers, prosecutors, defense attorneys, licensing authorities, and public and private placements. State and local laws, police practices, and judicial orders create the framework for decisions about admission and release. As a result, detention managers do not directly control these decisions and cannot predict with precision the number of clients their programs will serve. Yet the ability to control and predict the resident population, at least to some degree, is critical.

Clarity of mission is a first step toward gaining a measure of control.

In a changing environment, a clear definition of purpose can be a stabilizing force. Just as important is a forum for cooperation and communication between detention and those agencies which affect it. These two features, clear purpose and effective communication, lay the groundwork for the relationship between detention and its external environment.

As in any organization, in juvenile detention clarity of mission is critical. Fully and clearly defined purposes become the foundation for decisions and coherent policies. In broad terms, the mission of detention is to provide temporary custody for juveniles accused of delinquent acts from the time of their arrest until the court reaches a disposition. This definition is a starting place, but it is not a good mission statement. It is vague and bland; it has no philosophical content and provides no direction. A strong mission statement, one with power to shape an organization, includes beliefs and values as well as expectations about what will happen to detained juveniles between arrest and disposition.

In 1990, the National Juvenile Detention Association (NJDA) adopted a definition of juvenile detention that captures its essence (Stokes and Smith, 1990):

> Juvenile detention is the temporary and safe custody of juveniles who are accused of conduct subject to the jurisdiction of the court and require a restricted environment for their own community's safety while pending legal action.
>
> Further, juvenile detention provides a wide range of helpful services that support the juvenile's physical, emotional, and social development. Helpful services minimally include: education, recreation, counseling, nutrition, medical and health care services, reading, visitation, communication, and continuous supervision. Juvenile detention includes or provides for a system of clinical observation and assessment that complements the helpful services and reports findings.

At the detention center in Pittsburgh and through Pennsylvania's professional association, I sought to construct a coherent mission statement which was consistent with the NJDA definition and which combined legal mandates with a passion for excellence. Ideas from practitioners and the literature on detention formed the basis for a two-part statement. The first part establishes philosophical principles; the second part defines purposes. The resulting mission statement, reproduced here, is rooted in the law and reaches for quality in services.

The Mission of Juvenile Detention

Juvenile detention's mission rests on five principles:

1. Respect for the dignity of the human person is basic.
2. Detention has responsibility to both the community and the offender; detention must protect public safety but should be restricted so that only those needing it are held, and for as short a period as possible.
3. Although detention is designed to be brief, it is a time of crisis and uncertainty when the quality of human relationships is more important than the duration.
4. Because juveniles are immature and still developing, the impact of environment is forceful. No environment is neutral; it either fosters development or damages it.
5. The aims of detention must be consistent with those of the larger juvenile justice system, including the court, probation, and corrections.

In keeping with these principles, secure custody is basic. But mere custody ignores the needs of human dignity and adolescent development, as well as the conditions of uncertainty and crisis. Detention cannot offer treatment in a traditional sense; the stay is short, and the need for treatment cannot be assumed for youths who have not yet had a hearing. Neither custody nor treatment is an adequate concept when applied to detention; elements of each are required for a complete view. Secure detention should be organized and operated to promote security and thus protect the community, but it should also foster the physical, intellectual, social, and emotional development of its residents. This conclusion is the basis for defining five purposes:

1. Secure Custody. Secure custody is prevention of escapes and intrusions. It relies on observation, supervision, and control of residents, and on design and maintenance of the physical plant.
2. Safety. Safety is protection of residents from physical and emo-

tional harm. It is accomplished through supervision and through reporting and managing suspected abuse, emergencies, and issues related to physical plant maintenance.

3. Health and Well-Being. Medical screening, routine care, emergency treatment, and nutrition are basic health services. Promoting resident knowledge of health issues and affording opportunities for mental health guidance are also elements of health and well-being.

4. Observation, Assessment, and Reporting. Detention gathers educational, psychological, and social information to aid resident adjustment and to report to the court and to placement agencies.

5. Resident Development. Detention develops knowledge, skills, attitudes, and behavior through incentives and discipline, formal programs, and the informal climate. The aims of resident development are to enhance self-esteem and impart a sense of responsibility; to teach academic and social skills; and to offer opportunities for physical training, recreation, and expression of thoughts and feelings in a climate of encouragement and fairness.

In a few words, the mission of detention is *to provide safe, secure custody and to promote the health and well-being of youths committed to its care, in an environment that fosters physical, intellectual, social, and emotional development.* No program will be effective in managing the external environment or internal operations without a grasp of its own purposes. Once the mission is clear, the challenge is to translate ideas into practice.

The first step is to resolve issues at the boundary between detention and its environment, such as admission criteria, case monitoring, and release policies. From the experience of developing a program, I have identified seven features that promote the control and predictability so essential to making detention work in its relationship to an uncertain environment. Detention managers have limited control over these features. Most depend on the decisions of legislators, judges, and elected officials. Detention administrators need to manage the elements that they can control and then set out to influence those they cannot. The features at the boundary between detention and its environment can be developed and managed effectively only to the extent that various components of the system cooperate and communicate with each other and share a common vision about the purposes of detention. The seven elements are the following:

Information

Planning for an adequate number of beds in a jurisdiction depends on ability to project needs. Reliable statistics on population trends, delinquency rates, and demographic factors allow for planning in order to avoid chronic overcrowding that can undermine good programs. Although detention managers can keep and gather information, their control of this element is only moderate. A reliable information system requires the cooperative efforts of all components of the larger system. Nevertheless, detention managers need to take initiative in analyzing and disseminating data as a basis for planning and for advocating for admission criteria and case review.

A Standard of Separation

Federal standards prohibit housing adults and status offenders in juvenile detention centers. Although they have not been universally adopted, implementing these standards reduces the chances of overcrowding and is faithful to the mission of detention. Acceptance of a separation is not in the hands of detention managers; it is a matter of government and court policy. But detention managers can individually and collectively influence policymakers.

Admission Criteria

Unambiguous jurisdictional standards must address ages of clients to be served, geographic limits of service, and kinds of offenses that constitute eligibility for admission. Criteria for admission need to be precise, complete, and balanced in order to protect the public while offering a degree of predictability. Examples of criteria currently in place in Pennsylvania include (Pennsylvania Juvenile Court Judges' Commission, 1986):

The child is alleged to be a delinquent child on the basis of acts which would constitute the commission of, conspiracy, solicitation, or an attempt to commit: criminal homicide, rape, robbery, (or other specified felonies).

The child is alleged to be a delinquent child on the basis of an offense which is classified as a felony and has been found to be a delinquent child within the preceding 18 months.

The child is an absconder from an institution or other placement to which he or she was committed as a result of a previous adjudication of delinquency.

The child has willfully failed to appear at a hearing on the petition (adjudication hearing) or other hearing after having been served with a court order or summons to appear.

Admission standards should address use of detention as a disposition. When detention is used as a placement or for punishment, the integrity of its mission may be compromised. If the decision is made to use detention in this way, clear guidelines for how that should happen need to be in place so that programs can be designed to recognize the difference between juveniles awaiting disposition and those serving a disposition.

Setting admission criteria is outside direct control of detention managers, but they can take an active role in advocating for them.

Judicial Review

A mechanism for prompt judicial review of detention decisions is a source of control and predictability. Such a mechanism compensates for the absence of a right to bail for juveniles and increases the likelihood of adherence to admission criteria. In Pennsylvania, a detention hearing is required within 72 hours of a juvenile's admission. Many jurisdictions in the state strive to meet a more ideal standard of 24 hours.

Detention Alternatives

Some juveniles require less structure than exists in secure detention but more structure than they have when they are free to roam the community. Juveniles in this category often end up in secure detention because no alternative exists. Detention managers have a measure of control in this area. Alternatives are often less costly than secure detention. In conjunction with judges and court managers, detention administrators can determine the need for alternatives, and establish shelter care, home detention, and day programming.

Timely Disposition and Release

Time limitations on hearings and dispositions are in keeping with the intent that detention extend over as short a period as possible. In

Pennsylvania, petitions must be filed within 24 hours, and hearings must be held within ten days of a juvenile's admission. Court reviews must be held every twenty days thereafter. A speedy court process builds control and accountability. But it relies on the availability of an adequate range of placements so that dispositions can be carried out without delay. Otherwise, juveniles linger in detention. Detention managers do not control the timing of disposition and release, but they can influence policymakers through legislative advocacy, joint review of policy and individual cases with the court, and informal persuasion.

Case Monitoring

In addition to standards for prompt and frequent judicial review, detention and probation managers need to provide for joint administrative review of juveniles in detention. They need to be constantly aware of the status of each detainee and unceasingly ask questions aimed at ensuring that everything is being done to expedite each case. These questions should address the scheduling of court cases, mechanisms for placement referral, responses by placement agencies, the efficiency of medical and psychological assessment resources, and the availability of transportation. Obstacles to timely transfer or release need to be frequently and systematically scrutinized. Detention managers can exercise a high level of control over case monitoring.

In summary, seven elements at the boundary between detention and its environment lay the groundwork for effective operations: reliable information, separation of adults and juveniles, admission criteria, judicial review, detention alternatives, timely disposition, and continual case monitoring. These features do not guarantee a model program, but taken together they offer a framework for stability. They help identify the client population and establish accountability for decisions that are in accord with the purposes of detention.

Managing relationships at the boundary between detention and its environment may be the central task facing practitioners. It takes precedence over internal management because success at the boundary is an essential condition for quality of program. Since it is a prerequisite for quality, jurisdictions that seek to move toward the model detention program need to start here. Overcrowding, inappropriate use of detention, lack of resources—consequences of problems between detention and the larger environment—undermine the best-designed programs.

Managers need to actively address issues at the local level and at the larger levels of state, nation, and society. This may seem too big an order, but the task is not impossible. The way to meet the challenge is to build coalitions.

Building coalitions means making connections with individuals, groups, organizations, and agencies that can make a difference or who believe that they have a stake in the future of detention. Networking, sensitivity to stakeholders, attention to constituencies—these are other names for coalition building. Sometimes a coalition is forged through formal means: reports on the goals, accomplishments, and shortcomings of the detention center; speeches and brochures that interpret the philosophy and purposes of the program; tours and educational events that open the facility to the community; advisory boards and public meetings that involve key actors from the outside. Just as often coalition building is achieved informally: responsiveness to inquiries from the community; sensitive handling of telephone calls and letters from parents, victims, and concerned citizens; regular and cordial contacts with judges, legislators, and other key decision makers so that positive relationships are firmly in place when crises arise. Informal relationships and the role of trust between key players should not be underestimated. The right word at the right time by a trusted manager can convince a judge to take action to relieve overcrowding or a sheriff to transport a resident to placement. It is critical that managers nurture informal channels and build trust through a record of performance, honesty, and respect.

Both formal and informal relationships demand skills in listening and language. A good listener responds with the same words the speaker is using. A distraught victim wants to hear words that show understanding of his or her sadness and anger. Sensitive use of language pays attention to the audience. A community group frightened by rising crime wants to hear about "security" and "public safety." It wants to know about measures for "preventing escapes" and "holding kids responsible." University students might want to know about "counseling techniques" and "educational programs." Language is a means of bridging differences and building coalitions. Although language may need to change with the audience, honesty should never be sacrificed. After all, the key to coalition building is trust.

The examples of coalition building presented so far apply at the local level, but the process is just as critical on the larger stage. Detention practitioners can build coalitions with one another, with representatives from other parts of the juvenile justice system and from different levels of government, with the research and academic community, and with leaders of churches, businesses, corporations, and foundations. The American Correctional Association, the National Juvenile Detention Association, and state professional associations are examples of potentially strong coalitions. In Pennsylvania, the Department of Public Welfare appointed a juvenile justice task force with representatives from every component of the system and charged them with responsibility for a thorough review. The Juvenile Detention Centers Association of Pennsylvania was awarded a quarter million dollars in grants to conduct statewide training for detention staff. Coalitions with focus and purpose can make changes.

To move toward purposeful and constructive change on a large scale requires bold action by practitioners who understand that issues facing juvenile detention need to be brought into the public forum. Detention practitioners need to abandon traditional secrecy, openly address issues, marshal research on critical questions, and act to bring about change (Roush, 1990). Social scientists need to conduct competent qualitative and quantitative research on key issues: does sentencing to detention change or impair the ability to deliver programs; how does crowding affect quality of life; what program issues should be addressed to more effectively deal with the increasing proportion of minorities (Roush, 1990, p. 9). Opportunities for research can be nurtured through links between detention and higher education. Collaboration with higher education also promises the mutual benefits of field trips, internships, and staff recruitment and development.

Management education is one aspect of staff development that collaboration and coalition building can enhance. The day-to-day management skills of budgeting, goal setting, communication, and conflict resolution can be developed. And the training managers can move beyond these traditional skills to cultivate the broader capabilities of leadership, vision, and strategic planning. Managing detention at the boundary requires qualities that acknowledge the place of detention in a complex social system. Without acceding to the myth that business is better managed than government and human services, detention managers need to explore the best that is offered in business theory and practice.

Excellent training and material is available to detention practitioners from the worlds of business and education. Mintzberg (1973) published a classic study of management work that identified ten roles under three headings: Interpersonal Roles—figurehead, leader, liaison; Informational Roles—monitor, disseminator, spokesman; Decisional Roles—entrepreneur, disturbance handler, resource allocator, negotiator. The Wharton School teaches valuable management tools. Some examples are:

> *Stakeholder Mapping*: All organizations are influenced by internal and external stakeholders. Stakeholder Mapping is a technique to assess the potential impact of all stakeholders on a set of organizational objectives, or a specific plan of action. This information provides a foundation upon which to build strategies to manage stakeholder relations.
>
> *Nominal Group Technique*: Meetings within organizations are not always productive. Most managers feel that much of their time . . . in meetings is not well spent. Nominal Group Technique is a way of organizing a meeting to enhance its productivity. Its purpose is to balance and increase participation, to use different processes for different phases of creative problem solving and to reduce the errors . . . in group decisions. It is especially useful for problem identification, problem solving, and program planning.
>
> *Responsibility Charting*: As organizations become more complex, the quality of inter-unit relationships often deteriorates . . . Responsibility charting is a structured process for surfacing different perceptions and jointly negotiating clear agreements. These agreements and the process of achieving them can improve accountability, effective delegation, and communications.
>
> *Scanning the Environment*: Managers are usually preoccupied with internal issues . . . They often fail to identify and appreciate issues and ideas outside of their organization. Scanning the environment encourages a group to look outside of their narrow organizational boundaries at the wider environment. During this process managers identify ideas that are becoming powerful for action, ideas that are beginning to dominate public debate and affect the flow of funds. They can develop strategies to adapt to the changing circumstances (Wharton School, unpublished manuscript).

These are four tools among many available to enterprising managers who seek to shape the future. Another concept that promises to move organizations to new levels of accomplishment is "total quality management," a process designed to eliminate error in the workplace and involve all staff in the pursuit of excellence (Crosby, 1984). Management skills and tools, combined with vision, offer the best hope for progress: "*Vision* . . . is a 'see' word. It evokes images and pictures. Visual metaphors are very common when we are talking about long range plans . . . (*V*)*ision* suggests a future orientation (and) an image of the future . . . (*V*)*ision* connotes a standard of excellence, an ideal" (Kouzes and Posner, 1987).

In addition to developing and expressing their own visions, strong leaders are willing to look outside traditional boundaries and explore new ways of seeing things. For example, detention practitioners are used to looking for resources from government. But staying within this view may limit them in solving problems and blind them to possibilities, such as resources from private corporations and foundations. Meeting the challenges of the future will require vision, risk, and bold exploration.

Clarity of purpose, coalition building, vision—these are fundamental to successfully managing relationships at the boundary between detention and an uncertain, changing environment. They are also keys to successful internal management. The purposes of secure custody, safety, health and well-being, and resident assessment and development govern every aspect of work performed in detention. Coalitions among work units, and between management and line staff, are critical for success. A vision, shared in common and translated into practice, becomes a driving force.

Supervision, care, and development constitute the primary responsibilities of detention. The work that directly promotes the purposes of detention includes observing, supervising, counseling, and teaching residents. It also includes admitting and orienting new clients, providing health care and food service, and overseeing recreation and parental visits. These activities are the heart of the detention operation.

Among the elements of quality direct care are: adequate ratio of staff to residents; meeting basic needs; clarity about rights and responsibilities; prevention and control of dangerous behavior; and effective programs. The following describes each of these points in greater detail:

1. *Staff to Resident Ratio.* An adequate number of qualified staff must be present to meet the goals of security, safety, health, and development. There is no magic number for determining staff-to-resident ratio. In Pennsylvania, a ratio is mandated: one direct care staff for every 6 residents during waking hours and one for every 12 during sleeping hours. The aim is for staff to be able to see and hear residents with ease. The mandated ratio for direct care staff is adequate, if supervisors, teachers, and support staff are also present. The full complement in Pittsburgh provides a ratio of one to four.

2. *Meeting Basic Needs.* Shelter, food, and clothing are basic human needs. Also basic are provisions for health, hygiene, and comfort. Access to recreation and outdoor activities is important. Finally, the opportunity for contact with family and attorney through personal visits, letters, and telephone calls is a basic human right. Meeting basic needs is a direct sign of respect for human dignity and vitally affects each individual's sense of well-being and the level of control in the environment.

3. *Rights and Responsibilities.* A sound detention program has clear written policies on the rights and responsibilities of both staff and residents. Rules and expectations must be communicated to residents through an orientation program. Residents must be informed of rewards and consequences as well as appeal procedures.

4. *Behavior Management.* A consistently applied system of incentives and discipline is essential. Also important are policies, procedures, and standards to prevent and control behavior that threatens security and safety: search, isolation, physical restraint, and crisis intervention.

5. *Programs.* Formal programs are purposeful, structured activities built on stated objectives: group discussion, plays and skits, role play, and classroom activities. Subjects might include reading, chemical dependency, nutrition, careers, sexually transmitted disease, arts and crafts, physical fitness, and decision-making. Informal programs take place in small ways every day when staff create, discover, and take advantage of opportunities to help residents learn new knowledge, skills, attitudes, and behavior: respect for others, care of property, grooming, dealing with anger. Both formal and informal programs need to be rooted in goals and values shared by staff. Shuman Center uses a frame-

work of skills that focus on self-esteem and responsibility to others (Strayhorn, 1988). The skills are formulated as specific learning objectives appropriate to a detention setting. In theory, if every staff member teaches the same skills, consistency becomes characteristic and chances for residents to learn rise. The skills offer a common direction. They become themes for developing the residents—a blueprint for learning.

The five features of quality direct care are at the heart of a model juvenile detention program. Of equal importance are the support, resources, leadership, and commitment of detention management. Among the responsibilities of managers are four key tasks critical to establishing a successful program: development and communication of sound policies, procedures, and standards; acquisition, allocation, and monitoring of resources; selection, training, and development of staff; and evaluation of past performance and planning for future accomplishments. Each of these features of management work is described in detail.

Policies, Procedures, and Standards

Effective policies and procedures are clear and comprehensive. Clarity is achieved through simple, direct language that is free of jargon. Policies, procedures, and standards need to be easily available to staff, and the means of keeping them up to date need to be in place. A practical way of arriving at a comprehensive set of policies, procedures, and standards begins with the mission statement and asks what is required to meet the purposes contained in it. For example, the purpose of secure custody requires policies and procedures on search, firearms, keys and locks, and mechanical restraints. The purpose of safety requires policies and procedures on fire prevention and response, suspected abuse, and storage of hazardous materials. The American Correctional Association (ACA) Standards for Juvenile Detention are a source for identifying policy and procedure requirements (American Correctional Association, 1983). The ACA has also published a compendium of model policies and procedures, some of which originated at Shuman Center in Pittsburgh (American Correctional Association, 1984). Good policies and procedures are important, but they are empty unless they are communicated, discussed, interpreted, and, most important of all, practiced.

Resource Management

Building a successful program requires a high level of management performance in acquiring, allocating, and monitoring resources. The physical plant and operating funds are the primary resources. Anyone who works in a poorly designed or maintained facility knows how important the physical plant is to meeting the purposes of detention. The building and grounds have direct implications for security, safety, health, and development. A few design axioms are generally accepted: large groups in confined space create tension; provisions for small groups and some privacy reduce tension; private rooms serve safety and ease behavior management; resident services on one floor is an advantage, eliminating elevators and stairs. Recreation space and access to the outdoors are classic requirements. Materials for and placement of bathrooms, doors, locks, and fire exits are of great importance. Design and maintenance must acknowledge the relationship space has with the accomplishment of organizational purposes.

Adequate funding is the second resource. Funding sources, governing bodies, and the public must be willing to pay the cost of security, safety, health, and well-being. Detention managers have the responsibility to define what constitutes adequate funding and to make the case for its allocation. They have the corresponding responsibility to manage those funds with rigorous efficiency and integrity.

Staff Selection and Development

Competent, caring staff is more important than any element in creating a model program and achieving the mission of detention. Management performs no more important tasks than selecting and training staff. Selection is a key management decision, and it must be tied to mission. The goal is to recruit and hire persons possessed of the knowledge and skills required to achieve the mission. Managers must also find employees of character who are committed to young people. Traditional means of discovering a candidate's potential are useful: interviews, tests, references, background checks, on-the-job observation, and probationary periods. Education, experience, and skill are, of course, factors in selection; but no less important are the more elusive qualities of honesty, integrity, courage, and capacity for teamwork. Qualities of character are not easy to predict. Closely supervised probation offers the best chance to learn about them. Low pay and high stress are obstacles to recruitment and retention that can be overcome only by commitment to employee rights and rewards and by translating commitment into humane scheduling practices, job enrichment, recognition of performance, employee participation in policy-making, and opportunities for training and professional development.

Training builds morale and is also a means of translating mission into practice. It is a primary force in making a model program. Training is an extension of selection. The hiring process seeks to discover people with certain skills and at the same time to educate candidates about the job. Training develops skills already present and expands understanding of the aims of the organization. Successful training meets several requirements:

1. Someone is responsible—a training director or the employee's supervisor—but at the same time all staff see themselves as assisting in training, and the environment supports learning as a primary value.
2. Orientation is provided to newly hired employees during the first eighty hours of employment. The orientation has clear objectives, a definite curriculum, and the means to ensure that learning has occurred.
3. A comprehensive training program for all staff is provided. Following an ingenious schedule designed at the San Antonio Detention Center (Kossman, 1990), eight hours of training is provided each month. Rather than covering piecemeal topics, the content connects directly to the mission and to job responsibilities, and is specified in a coherent curriculum.
4. Verification that learning objectives have been met is important. It is not enough for training to occur; *learning* is the goal. Training is not accomplished when a session is held and documented in employee records; it is accomplished when learning occurs and is verified. A certification test is one way of measuring learning.
5. The total environment must support learning—in supervisory conferences, in job performance evaluations, and in every interaction among staff. Training is more than a program; it is a process that never ends.

In addition to training, recognition of performance and participation in policy decisions contribute to staff development. Excellent work performance should be acknowledged publicly and often. Access to means of shaping policy is equally important. At the detention center in Pittsburgh, any employee can participate in regular meetings in three policy areas: safety and security, resident programs, and human resources. Employees shape the meeting agenda and affect policy decisions. Acknowledgment of the staff's pivotal role will yield immeasurable benefits.

Evaluation and Planning

The basic management responsibilities of evaluation and planning are two sides of the same coin. Evaluation asks how well the organization is doing; planning asks what the organization can do to be better in the future. Both are based on an understanding of what constitutes organization performance.

Organization performance is success in five areas:

1. The organization's relationship to its environment: how effective is the relationship with the court and with placement agencies; are admission criteria in place and respected; can some measure of control and predictability be exercised over admissions?
2. Acquisition and use of resources: is the organization able to capture and retain financial and human resources; is the building adequate in size and to what extent does it serve the purposes of safety, security, health, and development; is funding adequate and managed efficiently; is the staff structured, scheduled, and assigned work effectively?
3. Internal processes: how many clients are being served; do activities support goals; how well do support services such as purchasing, cooking, and clerical work function?
4. Achievement of purposes and goals: are the purposes of safety, security, health, and development being met; to what extent are there escapes, injuries, assaults, or other indicators of performance failure?
5. Satisfaction of clients and employees: to what extent do residents and staff feel safe; do residents feel that the staff care about them; do employees show signs of trust, respect, and loyalty; what is the state of employee morale; how effective are processes for

communication, problem solving, and conflict resolution among individuals and groups; to what degree are opportunities for innovation, self expression, and autonomy afforded?

Detention managers need to find ways of gathering information and measuring achievement in all five of these areas. Information on these five performance dimensions becomes a powerful tool for planning and for shaping a model juvenile detention program.

Conclusion

Secure juvenile detention is a necessary component of juvenile justice. Because it is a time of crisis and uncertainty, even a brief period in detention is of great significance to residents. Because detention directly affects public safety, it is of great importance to the community as well. Given the pivotal place of detention and its influence on so many lives—children, parents, victims—attention must be paid so that programs operate at the highest level of performance. Features that promote performance, excellence, and quality services have been described and can be summarized in a concise conceptual model:

Mission

1. Respect for dignity of human persons is basic.
2. Responsibility extends to both the community and the offender.

Principles

1. Detention is a brief, but critical, time.
2. The impact of environment on adolescents is forceful.
3. The aims of detention must be consistent with those of the larger juvenile justice system.

Purposes

Secure Custody, Safety, Health and Well-Being, and Resident Assessment and Development.

Standards at the Boundary Between Detention and Its Environment

1. Complete and accurate information base.
2. Separation of adults and juveniles.

3. Criteria for admission with the force of law.
4. Prompt judicial review of detention decisions.
5. Availability of detention alternatives, such as shelter and in-home detention.
6. Timely disposition and release.
7. Constant case monitoring.

Standards For Resident Care, Supervision, and Development

1. Adequate ratio of staff to residents.
2. Meeting basic needs: food, shelter, clothing, and health.
3. Clarity about rights and responsibilities of both staff and residents.
4. Prevention and control of dangerous behavior.
5. Effective programs.

Standards For Management

1. Development and communication of clear and comprehensive policies, procedures, and standards.
2. Effective acquisition, allocation, and use of resources.
3. Sound processes for selecting, training, and developing staff.
4. Effective processes for organization evaluation and planning.

Accomplishment is always a matter of degree. The features described here are an ideal. No detention program can achieve all of them all the time. Not all of the features can be directly controlled, and there are many obstacles to putting them in place. But with vision, energy, skill, and determination, they can be influenced, and the ideal can be approached. As long as juvenile detention is part of society's efforts to address delinquency, those responsible for it have the professional obligation to strive to make detention work and to seek quality and excellence. The features of a model detention program are guidelines for meeting those obligations.

Bibliography

American Correctional Association. (1983). *Standards for juvenile detention facilities*. Laurel, MD: American Correctional Association.
———. (1984). *Guidelines for the development of policies and procedures: Juvenile detention facilities*.

Crosby, P. (1984). *Quality without tears*. New York: New American Library.

Kossman, S. P. (1990, Fall). Staffing pattern dynamics: A new approach to old problems. *Journal for Juvenile Justice and Detention Services, 5*(2), 9–12.

Kouzes, J., & Posner, B. (1987). *Leadership challenge*. San Francisco: Jossey-Bass.

Mintzberg, H. (1973). *The nature of managerial work*. New York: Harper & Row.

Pennsylvania Juvenile Court Judges' Commission. (1986). *Standards governing the use of secure detention under the Juvenile Act*. Harrisburg, PA.

Roush, D. (1990, October). *Juvenile detention in the 1990s*. Paper presented at the meeting for the Midwestern Criminal Justice Association, Chicago, IL.

Stokes, T., & Smith, S. (1990, Fall). Juvenile detention: A nationally recognized definition. *Journal for Juvenile Justice and Detention Services*, 24–26.

Strayhorn, J. M. (1988). *The competent child*. New York: Guilford Press.

The Wharton School. Management and Behavioral Science Center. Training materials on Scanning the Environment, Responsibility Charting, Nominal Group Technique, and Stakeholder Mapping.

7

Secure Detention in Pennsylvania, 1981–1990: The Experience after *Coleman v. Stanziani*

JAMES E. ANDERSON
AND ROBERT G. SCHWARTZ

By the spring of 1991, Pennsylvania had spent 10 years transforming the way it uses secure detention for juvenile offenders. The process began in 1981, when the Juvenile Law Center (JLC) filed a class-action lawsuit challenging the state's law and practice of preventive detention; the process took hold in 1985, when the state's Juvenile Court Judge's Commission (JCJC) took an active part in settling the litigation and in developing new detention standards for Pennsylvania. New standards were introduced in 1986 as part of the settlement of the litigation. JCJC has collected comprehensive detention data in the process of monitoring compliance with the consent decree and insuring its implementation.

The Pennsylvania experience suggests that the use of secure detention can be minimized without a resulting impact on crime rate. It further suggests that JCJC's participation in the crafting of the settlement and in monitoring its implementation has created a culture in which secure detention retains an important, but more clearly defined, role in the state's juvenile justice system.

The Lawsuit

Coleman v. Stanziani (No. 81–2215, ED Pa.) was filed in 1981 as a federal court class action challenging the constitutionality of §6325 of the Pennsylvania Juvenile Act, 42 Pa.C.S. §6325, which permitted the secure detention of a child when it was "required to protect the person or property of others or of the child or because the child may abscond or be removed from the jurisdiction . . ."

The named plaintiffs were two juveniles who were arrested in a stolen car and held in secure detention pending their adjudicatory hearings.[1] Representing a plaintiff class of allegedly delinquent Pennsylvania juveniles, they complained, *inter alia*, that Pennsylvania law was unduly vague, which led to its arbitrary application. Defendants were Pennsylvania's Juvenile Court judges and juvenile probation officers, who also had authority under Pennsylvania law to order pre-trial detention (42 Pa.C.S. §6304).

The ambiguities of the case, which were made manifest by defeats suffered by each side in 1983–84, led to serious negotiation. In September 1983, the district court dismissed the defendants' motion to dismiss the complaint, 570 F.Supp. 679 (E.D. Pa. 1983), a decision which was affirmed by the Third Circuit Court of Appeals, 735 F.2d 118 (3d Cir. 1984), *cert. denied* 469 U.S. 1037 (1984). On the same day that the Third Circuit affirmed the district court, the U.S. Supreme Court decided *Schall v. Martin*, 467 U.S. 253 (1984), which upheld a New York detention statute similar to Pennsylvania's. Both parties, uncertain how the Pennsylvania scheme would be perceived by the federal courts, agreed to explore a negotiated agreement. The negotiation was also encouraged by the findings of the plaintiffs' expert witness, John Goldkamp, whose study of Pennsylvania detention practices, made possible through the plaintiffs' discovery, confirmed many of the plaintiffs' allegations about variations in Pennsylvania detention practice.

The Goldkamp Study

Goldkamp (1984) examined detention practices in six Pennsylvania counties on October 7, 1981. The study was aimed at drawing "inferences about the use of detention from description of the juveniles" in detention in the six counties, which were selected for their urban, suburban, and rural characteristics. Two hundred seventy-eight cases were examined for 87 items of descriptive information. The selection of the 1981 date, which was almost one year prior to the study, also permitted the collection of follow-up data.

The Goldkamp study showed wide variation in detention practices in the six counties. In five of the counties, more than half of the detained juveniles were held on felony-level charges; in one county only 36% were held for felonies. In one suburban county, 65% of the youths were held for crimes against persons; in another suburban county, only 18% were held for such offenses. Weapons, robbery, drug-related charges, and offenses involving injury to persons were relatively rare. In one rural county, 53% of the confined juveniles had never been previously arrested; except in Philadelphia county, the majority of confined juveniles had no prior arrests for crimes against persons.

Two Years Prior to Settlement

Two processes occurred during the roughly two years following the Supreme Court decision in *Schall* and the Third Circuit decision in *Coleman*. First, the parties undertook to negotiate a settlement. Second, the use of secure detention in the state continued the decline that had begun following the filing of *Coleman* in 1981.

Plaintiffs and defendants in early 1985 found a trusted mediator in Paul DeMuro, a former Pennsylvania Deputy Secretary who was responsible for state child welfare programs, including components of the juvenile justice system, and who had developed a private consultation practice after working for the National Council on Crime and Delinquency. DeMuro kept the negotiations moving, helped the parties define their interests, and pushed both sides towards a reasonable settlement.

At the same time, use of detention declined in Pennsylvania. In 1981, the year *Coleman* was filed, 25% of the total Juvenile Court dispositions involved the use of secure detention. In 1982 the percentage was 12%, in 1984 13%, and by 1987, one year after the *Coleman* settlement became effective, only 10% of the Juvenile Court cases involved the use of detention. Between 1982 and 1989, six detention centers closed in the state.

The Settlement

On April 18, 1986, the federal district court for the Eastern District of Pennsylvania approved the *Coleman* consent decree. The decree became effective on September 1, 1986 and will remain in effect until

August 31, 1996.[2] It controls admission to secure detention in every Pennsylvania county except Philadelphia, whose secure detention practices are governed by a separate federal consent decree.

The settlement is a two-part document. The first part is the substance of the consent decree, which will be immutable for ten years; the second part consists of Pennsylvania's detention standards. The decree requires judges and juvenile probation officers to give statements of reasons for pre-trial decisions to use secure detention and to consider the use of less restrictive alternatives. The decree also prohibits the use of secure detention solely because of an absent parent or guardian.

The most significant aspect of the settlement is the requirement that there be a statement of reasons for detention. With the exception of situations where secure detention is ordered by a court subsequent to a finding that a child has committed a delinquent act, a contemporaneous written statement of reasons and facts must accompany every decision to detain a child in secure detention made by a judge, juvenile court master, or juvenile probation officer.

This statement of reasons must specify that there is a reasonable basis to believe the child has committed the act for which he is being detained (in the case of judicial authorities, that probable cause exists) and that the child is not excluded from the jurisdiction of the Juvenile Court by age or any other reason; that the child's detention is permitted under the "Standards Governing the Use of Secure Detention Under The Juvenile Act" promulgated by the Juvenile Court Judges' Commission pursuant to the settlement; which alternatives to secure detention were considered and rejected; and the reason or reasons why secure detention is required and why alternatives are not appropriate.

When secure detention is ordered by a court after a child is found to have committed a delinquent act but prior to the court's determination that residential placement will be ordered at disposition, the court must also indicate on the record or in a court order why secure detention is required and why alternatives are not appropriate (see copies of the forms authorizing detention). Once the court has determined that residential placement will be ordered, or continued if previously ordered, no statement of reasons is required regarding the use of secure detention pending the use of such placement.

Although the Standards permit the use of secure detention in extraordinary and exceptional circumstances where a child is not detention-eligible on the basis of other standards, the statement of facts and

JCJC-D-1
(7/86)

IN THE COURT OF COMMON PLEAS _____ JUDICIAL DISTRICT

_____ COUNTY

STATEMENT OF FACTS AND REASONS ACCOMPANYING THE DETENTION OF A CHILD
BY A PROBATION OFFICER/INTAKE OFFICER PURSUANT TO 42 PA. C. S. § § 6304, 6225, and 6331.

I.   Name of Child: _____   II. Date of Birth: _____ / _____ / _____
                    (Last)   (First)   (Middle Initial)   (Month) (Day) (Year)

III. Date Detention Authorized _____ / _____ / _____   IV. Time Of Authorization: _____ : _____ □ AM □ PM
                               (Month)   (Day)   (Year)

V.   There is a reasonable basis to believe that the above named child:

     A. □ has committed:

        1. ____ count(s) of (____) _____   4. ____ count(s) of (____) _____
                                        crime   crime

        2. ____ count(s) of (____) _____   5. ____ count(s) of (____) _____
                                        crime   crime

        3. ____ count(s) of (____) _____   6. ____ count(s) of (____) _____
                                        crime   crime

           If more than six crimes are alleged, list the six most serious crimes. In the parentheses (____), provide the code letter for the type of
           crime as follows:
                                        a = the crime of   c = solicitation to commit
                                        b = an attempt to commit   d = conspiracy to commit

     B. □ Other (explain) _____
        _____
        _____

VI. This child is not believed to be excluded from the jurisdiction of Juvenile Court by age or any other reason.

VII. This child's detention is permitted and authorized pursuant to Section(s) _____ of the "Standards Governing the Use of Secure
     Detention Under The Juvenile Act" as set forth in the JCJC Detention Handbook.

VIII. The alternatives to secure detention which were considered and rejected: □ parent(s)/guardian(s) □ in-home detention □ relative(s)
      □ foster care   □ shelter care   □ other (specify) _____

IX. The reason or reasons why secure detention is required and alternatives are not appropriate: _____
     _____
     _____
     _____

     (If detention was authorized pursuant to Section 701 of the Standards, this statement must include an explanation of why an exception was
     warranted and why non-secure options were rejected.)

     Name of Probation Officer/Intake Officer Authorizing Detention:

     Print Name: _____ Signature _____ Date: _____ / _____ / _____
                 (Last)   (First)   (Middle Initial)   (Month) (Day) (Year)

     Send WHITE AND YELLOW COPIES of this form, completed through Section IX, to the Detention Center within one court business day of this child's admission to
     detention.

To Be Completed by Detention Staff After Child's Admission to Detention:

X.   Name of Detention Center _____   XI. Date of admission of above named child: _____ / _____ / _____
                                                                                                           (Month) (Day) (Year)
                              □ A.M.
XII. Time of Admission: _____ : _____ □ P.M.

XIII. Detention/Release Status:
                                                                                                                          □ A.M.
     A. □ Child released prior to informal detention hearing: Date of Release _____ / _____ / _____ Time of Release _____ : _____ □ P.M.
                                                                              (Month) (Day)   (Year)
                                                                                                                          □ A.M.
     B. □ Child released at informal detention hearing: Date of Release _____ / _____ / _____ Time of Release _____ : _____ □ P.M.
                                                                        (Month) (Day)   (Year)

     C. □ Child continued in detention following informal detention hearing: Date of Detention Hearing _____ / _____ / _____
                                                                                                        (Month) (Day)   (Year)

     D. □ Other (explain) _____

     Name of Detention Center Staff Completing This Section:

     Print Name _____ Date: _____ / _____ / _____
                (Last)   (First)   (Middle Initial)   (Month) (Day) (Year)

Complete Sections X.-XIII. upon the child's release from detention or following the informal detention hearing, whichever occurs first. Send completed WHITE
COPY to the JUVENILE COURT JUDGES' COMMISSION (P.O. Box 1234, Federal Square Station, Harrisburg, PA 17108) with the Monthly Detention Summary
(JCJC-D-3) which reports this child's admission to detention.

-48-

JCJC-D-2
(7/86)

IN THE COURT OF COMMON PLEAS _____ JUDICIAL DISTRICT

_____ COUNTY

☐ STATEMENT OF FACTS AND REASONS ACCOMPANYING THE DETENTION/CONTINUED DETENTION OF A CHILD BY A JUDGE OR MASTER PRIOR TO ADJUDICATION

☐ ORDER OF COURT AUTHORIZING DETENTION/CONTINUED DETENTION OF A CHILD PRIOR TO ADJUDICATION

I. Name of Child: _____   II. Date of Birth: _____/_____/_____
        (Last)   (First)   (Middle Initial)   (Month)   (Day)   (Year)

III. Type of Proceeding/Order:
        ☐ Informal Detention Hearing pursuant to 42 PA. C.S. § 6332   ☐ Order of Court/no hearing
        ☐ Hearing To Continue Pre-adjudication Detention pursuant
            to 42 PA.C.S. § 6335

IV. Detention Center: _____   V. Date Of Admission to Detention: _____/_____/_____
                                                                                                    (Month)   (Day)   (Year)

VI. It has been determined that probable cause exists that the above named child:

        A. ☐ has committed:

            1. ____ count(s) of (____) _____   4. ____ count(s) of (____) _____
                                            crime   crime

            2. ____ count(s) of (____) _____   5. ____ count(s) of (____) _____
                                            crime   crime

            3. ____ count(s) of (____) _____   6. ____ count(s) of (____) _____
                                            crime   crime

            If more than six crimes are alleged, list the six most serious crimes. In the parentheses (____) provide the code letter for the type of
            crime as follows: a = the crime of   c = solicitation to commit
                                            b = an attempt to commit   d = conspiracy to commit

        B. ☐ Other (explain) _____
            _____
            _____

VII. This child is not believed to be excluded from the jurisdiction of Juvenile Court by age or any other reason.

VIII. This child's detention is permitted and authorized pursuant to Section(s) _____ of the "Standards Governing the Use of Secure Detention under the Juvenile Act" as set forth in the JCJC Detention Handbook.

IX. The alternatives to secure detention which were considered and rejected: ☐ parent(s)/guardian(s)   ☐ in-home detention   ☐ relative(s)
        ☐ foster care   ☐ shelter care   ☐ other (specify) _____

X. The reason or reasons why secure detention is required and alternatives are not appropriate: _____
        _____
        _____

(If detention was authorized pursuant to Section 701 of the Standards, this statement must include an explanation of why an exception was warranted and why non-secure options were rejected.)

_____   _____
                Judge/Master   Date
(No signature or date needed here if Order of Court entered below)

IN THE INTEREST OF: _____   No. _____
                                                A MINOR

        DOB: _____   **ORDER OF COURT**

    AND NOW, This _____ day of _____, 19____, (☐ a hearing having been held)

    it is hereby   ☐ ORDERED   ☐ RECOMMENDED

    that the above named child be detained in the _____ until further Order of this Court.
                                                                        Detention Center

RECOMMENDED: _____   BY THE COURT:
                                    Master

Subject to Approval by and further Order of this Court.

APPROVED: _____/_____/_____
                    Mo.   Day   Yr.

        BY THE COURT: _____
                                                                                            Judge

        _____
                    Judge

Send completed YELLOW AND PINK COPIES of this form to the detention center within one court business day of the Order of Court committing child to detention. If a separate Order of Court is used attached YELLOW AND PINK COPIES of this form to detention center copy of ORDER.

Detention Center: Send YELLOW COPY to the JCJC. (P.O. Box 1234, Federal Square Station, Harrisburg, PA 17108) with the Monthly **Detention Summary** (JCJC-D-3) which reports this child's admission to detention.   -52-

reasons which accompany such detention decisions must include an explanation of why an exception was warranted and why non-secure options were rejected. The Consent Decree provides that detention under this section may not be authorized routinely or because non-secure alternatives do not exist in adequate numbers.

The second part of the settlement consists of the standards. The standards have the force of law, although JCJC, as noted below, may change the standards if JCJC provides appropriate notice to plaintiffs and publishes the standards through the state's regulatory process. JCJC has "coded" the standards to facilitate compliance and monitoring. (See appendix.) The standards provide judges and probation officers with definitions of who may be held in secure detention pre-trial, post-trial awaiting disposition, and post-disposition.

Role of the Juvenile Court Judges' Commission

Settlement in this case could not have been achieved without development of both the "Standards Governing the Use of Secure Detention Under the Juvenile Act," and a mechanism to monitor compliance with those Standards. In Pennsylvania there are no statewide Juvenile Court rules. Consequently, the concept of requesting the Juvenile Court Judges' Commission to establish detention standards as the basis for settlement became an attractive option.

The Commission consists of nine judges appointed by the Governor from a list of judges serving in the Juvenile Courts submitted by the Chief Justice of Pennsylvania. The agency is empowered to advise the Juvenile Court judges in Pennsylvania in all matters pertaining to the proper care and maintenance of delinquent children; to examine the administrative methods and procedures used in Juvenile Courts throughout the state; to establish standards and make recommendations to the courts; to examine personnel practices and employment standards used in probation offices in the Commonwealth; and to collect, compile, and publish such statistical and other data as may be needed to accomplish the reasonable and efficient administration of the juvenile courts in Pennsylvania.

Prior to this settlement, the Commission had developed standards governing a number of procedures and administrative matters within

Pennsylvania's Juvenile Court system. Therefore, the concept of developing standards governing detention was regarded as consistent with the Commission's prior experience in standards development. Although the members of the Juvenile Court Judges' Commission were initially apprehensive about the prospects of reaching settlement in this case, they were nevertheless interested in the concept of seeking a settlement as a means of insulating Pennsylvania's juvenile justice system from further intervention by the federal courts in the area of detention. At settlement, the Commission viewed the consent decree as a very favorable resolution of the litigation and believed that the requirement of a statement of facts and reasons for detention would enhance the Pennsylvania system. Although the Consent Decree made detention standards binding on all judges, masters, and juvenile probation officers, the content of those standards remains in the sole control of the Pennsylvania Juvenile Court judges through the Commission, and the standards can be amended if the need arises. At the time of settlement, the Commission believed strongly that its success would hinge on the effectiveness of the Commission and its staff in providing technical assistance, training juvenile justice staff, and continuously supporting the values which were the basis of the settlement.

Following settlement, JCJC held a series of regional training programs for judges, masters, and probation officers to explain the rationale for the settlement and to provide detailed training regarding the use of the standards in making detention decisions. JCJC continues to provide on-going technical assistance through a staff specialist whose primary responsibilities focus on detention issues.

The Consent Decree also obligated JCJC to assume significant responsibilities for monitoring compliance. The Commission, at a minimum, must provide for the collection of information of sufficient detail to enable the parties to determine, for each county, the degree of compliance with all aspects of the Consent Decree and Standards, as well as details regarding the application of the provisions of the Standards which govern "authorization for detention in cases of extraordinary and exceptional circumstances." During the first two years of the settlement, Commission staff provided bi-monthly reports to counsel concerning compliance with the Decree. JCJC now issues reports on a semi-annual basis. These responsibilities necessitated the development of standard forms for use by judges, masters, and probation officers when making detention decisions. In addition, standard forms were developed for use by juvenile detention centers, which also provide reports to our staff on a monthly basis.

Analysis of Data

The data collected by the Juvenile Court Judges' Commission pursuant to the settlement suggest that the rate at which detention admissions occur in Pennsylvania has increased since the settlement. In 1987, there were 20,769 juvenile delinquency dispositions in the Commonwealth (excluding Philadelphia) and 5,875 secure detention admissions, which may be expressed as a detention rate of 28.3%. However, it should be noted that individual juveniles may have had more than one detention admission during the year and may also have had more than one juvenile court disposition. In 1988, there were 6,943 juvenile detention admissions and 22,090 juvenile delinquency dispositions for a detention rate of 31.4%. In 1989, there were 7,493 detention admissions and 23,013 juvenile delinquency dispositions, for a detention rate of 32.6%. On the basis of these statistics, the rate of detention increased approximately 10.9% between 1987 and 1988 and approximately 3.6% between 1988 and 1989.

Annual detention admission rates[3] can also be expressed as a percentage of total juvenile population. In 1987, the Pennsylvania juvenile population, age 10 to 17, was estimated to be 1,138,509 (excluding Philadelphia). Using the detention admissions previously presented, the rate of detention admissions per 100,000 juveniles was 516 in 1987, rose to 610 in 1988, and to 658 in 1989. The rate increased 18.2% from 1987 to 1988 and 7.8% from 1988 to 1989.

The frequency of detention admissions for certain crimes decreased during the period 1987 to 1989 but increased dramatically for others. For example, there were 305 pre-adjudication detention admissions in 1987 based on robbery charges. This figure dropped to 270 in 1988 and to 211 in 1989. However, pre-adjudication detention admissions for aggravated assault were 296 in 1987, rose to 349 in 1988, and to 474 in 1989. Detention admissions involving a new felony charge where the individual was currently on probation involved 243 admissions in 1987, 296 admissions in 1988, and 456 admissions in 1989.

Particularly interesting are the increases in codes where the juvenile is detained because he or she presents an extraordinary risk to abscond, but is not otherwise detention-admissible under the standards. Detention under the Commission's 206 code (the child presents extraordinary circumstances requiring secure detention to prevent him or her from absconding) occurred in 795 cases in 1987, rose to 1,026 in 1988, and to 1,211 in 1989. Admissions under the 206 code involved drug violations in approximately 5% of the 1987 admissions, approximately 7% of the 1988 admissions, and approximately 16% of the 1989 admissions. Similarly, auto theft cases involving the 206 code occurred in 7% of the 206 admissions in 1987, 11% of the cases in 1988, and approximately 12% of the Section 206 admissions in 1989.

Also interesting is the increase which has occurred in the number of admissions admitted under Section 701 (the child is not otherwise eligible for secure detention pursuant to the preceding standards; however, the facts present extraordinary and exceptional circumstances which require the use of secure detention). When this code is used, the statement of reasons which accompanies the decision must include an explanation of why an exception was warranted and why non-secure options were rejected. In addition, the Standards specify that detention under this section may not be authorized routinely or because non-secure alternatives do not exist in adequate numbers but only in the exceptional and extraordinary case.

In 1987, 142 detention admissions involved Section Code 701. This rose to 294 cases in 1988, and dropped slightly to 286 cases in 1989. As was the case with the Section 206 codes, both drug law violations and auto theft played significant roles in the increased usage of these codes. In 1987, auto theft charges were involved in approximately 7% of the Section 701 admissions. In 1988, auto theft charges were involved in 21% of the 701 admissions, while in 1989, auto theft violations made up 8% of the Section 701 admissions. Drug law violations, on the other hand, made up 15% of the 1987 Section 701 admissions, 32% of the 1988 701 admissions, and 40% of the 1989 701 admissions.

It is important to note that the ability of the courts to utilize both the 206 code and the 701 code in auto theft and drug law violations has enabled the Juvenile Court Judges' Commission to avoid giving consideration to amending the standards to provide a specific code for certain types of auto theft and certain drug law violations involving sales, delivery, or possession with intent to deliver a controlled substance. Such a change would likely lead to a substantial increase in the use of secure detention for these offenses.

Conclusion

The *Coleman* litigation was a useful catalyst in elevating detention as an issue that required official attention and in describing the uneven uses of detention in Pennsylvania at the beginning of the decade. The litigation prompted Pennsylvania judges, probation, and other officials to examine their practices. While the litigation was pending, those officials substantially reduced the rate of detention in the state, and they closed nearly one quarter of the state's secure detention centers.

The use of Paul DeMuro as an expert mediator assisted the parties in finding common values and in developing standards that would provide the contours for a decade of Pennsylvania detention practice. The judges and probation officers who were responsible for implementing the settlement thus shared the values that were the settlement's underpinning.

Settlement of a lawsuit of this sort is often merely the beginning of protracted enforcement actions. The parties avoided such contention in this case by building in a six-month period of training and education before the standards became operative. Successful implementation was made possible by JCJC's willingness to train the state's Juvenile Court judges and probation officers, develop a detention handbook to ensure consistency in application of the standards, and assume responsibility for monitoring and correcting non-compliance with the *Coleman* standards.

The Pennsylvania experience is thus a model for changing state practice. Key to the model is the requirement of a statement of reasons and examination of alternatives to secure detention in every case prior to adjudication, as well as the requirement for judicial review every ten days for children remaining in detention. This model increased consistency in decision-making, resulted in fairer use of secure detention, and made secure detention practices consistent with the treatment philosophy on which the rest of Pennsylvania's juvenile justice system is based. To achieve that result, the parties relied heavily on the shared values and cooperation of the outside advocates and those inside the system charged with its fair and equitable operation.

Appendix

JUVENILE COURT JUDGES' COMMISSION

Standards Governing
the Use of
Secure Detention Under The Juvenile Act
42 Pa. C. S. §6301, et seq.

The Standards which follow are a coded and annotated version of the Juvenile Court Judges' Commission Standards which were promulgated pursuant to the settlement in **Coleman, et al. -vs- Stanziani, et al., CA No. 81-2215,** approved on April 18, 1986 in the United States District Court for the Eastern District of Pennsylvania.

These Standards do not differ substantively from those filed with the Court. However, only those provisions which relate specifically to detention eligibility have been included, certain of which were restructured or rephrased for the sake of clarity.

This version of the Standards was developed solely to facilitate compliance with the settlement in **Coleman.** In all cases where it is necessary to cite a specific provision of the Juvenile Court Judges' Commission **"Standards Governing the Use of Secure Detention Under The Juvenile Act,"** the relevant section of this document should be cited.

7/86

STANDARDS GOVERNING
THE USE OF
SECURE DETENTION UNDER THE JUVENILE ACT

(Coded and Annotated)

---

1. CIRCUMSTANCES UNDER WHICH SECURE DETENTION MAY BE AUTHORIZED ON THE BASIS OF AN ALLEGED OFFENSE OR ON THE BASIS OF AN ALLEGED OFFENSE AND THE CHILD'S CURRENT STATUS WITH THE COURT OR PRIOR RECORD:

The child is alleged to be a delinquent child on the basis of acts which would constitute the commission of, conspiracy, solicitation, or an attempt to commit:

Section

101   Criminal homicide (18 Pa. C.S. §2502, Murder ; §2503, Voluntary Manslaughter ; §2504, Involuntary Manslaughter).

102   Rape (18 Pa. C.S. §3121).

103   Robbery (18 Pa. C.S. §3701).

104   Aggravated assault (18 Pa. C.S. §2702).

105   Involuntary deviate sexual intercourse (18 Pa. C.S. §3123).

106   Kidnapping (18 Pa. C.S. §2901).

107   Arson (18 Pa. C.S. §3301).

108   Burglary involving a structure adapted for overnight accomodation (18 Pa. C.S. §3502).

109   Terroristic threats (18 Pa C.S. §2706).

110   Causing or risking catastrophe (18 Pa. C.S §3302).

111   Riot (18 Pa. C.S. §5501).

112   Felonious intimidation of witnesses or victims (18 Pa. C.S. §4952).

Note: The offense is a felony of the third degree if:

(1)   The actor employs force, violence or deception, or threatens to employ force or violence, upon the witness or victim or, with the requisite intent or knowledge upon any other person.

(2)   The actor offers any pecuniary or other benefit to the witness or victim or, with the requisite intent or knowledge, to any other person.

(3)   The actor's conduct is in furtherance of a conspiracy to intimidate a witness or victim.

(4)   The actor solicits another to or accepts or agrees to accept any pecuniary or other benefit to intimidate a witness or victim.

(5)   The actor has suffered any prior conviction for any violation of this title or any predecessor law hereto, or has been convicted, under any Federal statute or statute of any other state, of an act which would be a violation of this title if committed in this State.

Otherwise the offense is a misdemeanor of the second degree.

7/86

113 **Felonious** retaliation against witness or victim (18 Pa. C.S. § 4935)

Note: The offense is a felony of the third degree if:

(1) The actor employs force, violence or deception, or threatens to employ force or violence, upon the witness or victim or, with the requisite intent or knowledge upon any other person.

(2) The actor offers any pecuniary or other benefit to the witness or victim or, with the requisite intent or knowledge, to any other person.

(3) The actor's conduct is in furtherance of a conspiracy to intimidate a witness or victim.

(4) The actor solicits another to or accepts or agrees to accept any pecuniary or other benefit to intimidate a witness or victim.

(5) The actor has suffered any prior conviction for any violation of this title or any predecessor law hereto, or has been convicted, under any Federal statute or statute of any other state, of an act which would be a violation of this title if committed in this State.

Otherwise the offense is a misdemeanor of the second degree.

Section

114 The child is alleged to be a delinquent child on the basis of an offense which involved the use or possession of a firearm or explosives.

Note: An allegation of delinquency made solely on the basis of possession of a firearm or explosives can be the basis for ordering or authorizing detention under this section.

115 The child is alleged to be a delinquent child on the basis of an offense which involved the use but not mere possession of a deadly weapon other than a firearm or explosives, or an offense (other than mere possession) during which the child had in his possession a deadly weapon as defined at 18 Pa. C.S. § 2301.

Note: The mere possession of a firearm or explosives can be the basis for authorizing detention under Section 114.

Pursuant to 18 Pa. C.S. § 2301:

Deadly weapon. Any firearm, whether loaded or unloaded, or any device designed as a weapon and capable of producing death or serious bodily injury, or any other device or instrumentality which, in the manner in which it is used or intended to be used, is calculated to produce death or serious bodily injury.

Serious Bodily Injury. Bodily injury which creates a substantial risk of death or which causes serious, permanent disfigurement, or protracted loss or impairment of the function of any bodily member or organ.

116 The child is alleged to be a delinquent child on the basis of an offense which is classified as a felony and the child is currently on probation, being supervised under a Consent Decree, or is otherwise under the supervision of the Court following an adjudication of delinquency.

117 The child is alleged to be a delinquent child on the basis of an offense which is classified as a felony and the child has been found to be a delinquent child within the preceding 18 months.

118 The child is alleged to have committed **any delinquent act** and the child is on probation or is otherwise under the supervision of a Court following an adjudication of delinquency, **based on a felony.**

119 The child is on probation or is otherwise under the supervision of a Court following an adjudication of delinquency, **based on a felony,** and the child is alleged to have **twice violated technical conditions** of such probation or other post-adjudication supervision.

7/86

2. CIRCUMSTANCES UNDER WHICH SECURE DETENTION MAY BE AUTHORIZED ON THE BASIS OF A CHILD'S STATUS AS AN ABSCONDER OR FUGITIVE; ON THE BASIS OF A CHILD'S RECORD OF FAILING TO APPEAR AT PREVIOUS JUVENILE PROCEEDINGS; OR, BECAUSE OF EXTRAORDINARY CIRCUMSTANCES WHICH REQUIRE SECURE DETENTION TO PREVENT A CHILD FROM ABSCONDING:

Section

201   The child is an absconder from an institution or other placement to which he/she was committed as a result of a previous adjudication of delinquency.

202   The child has willfully failed to appear at the hearing on the petition (adjudication hearing) or other hearing after having been served with a court order or summons to appear.

203   The child has a recent demonstrable record of willful failure to appear at previous juvenile proceedings.

204   The child has been verified to be a fugitive from another jurisdiction, an official from which has requested that said child be detained.

205   The child absconded from shelter care or other non-secure placement ordered or authorized pending a court hearing or placement.

206   The child presents extraordinary circumstances requiring secure detention to prevent him/her from absconding. (Such circumstances may include, but are not limited to, the child's age, character, mental condition, drug or alcohol addiction or substance abuse.)

3. CIRCUMSTANCES UNDER WHICH SECURE DETENTION MAY BE AUTHORIZED ON THE WRITTEN REQUEST OF THE CHILD OR CHILD'S ATTORNEY:

Section

301   The child has voluntarily, and in writing, requested to be placed in secure detention for his/her protection.

   Note: Immediate release must occur upon the request of the child or child's attorney.

302   The child's attorney has voluntarily and in writing requested that the child be placed in secure detention for the protection of the child.

   Note: Immediate release must occur upon the request of the child or child's attorney.

7/86

4. CIRCUMSTANCES UNDER WHICH SECURE DETENTION MAY BE ORDERED PENDING DISPOSITION, SUBSEQUENT TO A FINDING THAT A CHILD COMMITTED A DELINQUENT ACT OR IS A DELINQUENT CHILD:

Section

401   The child was found to have committed a delinquent act, or adjudicated delinquent, on the basis of an offense for which detention was or could have been authorized or ordered pursuant to Sections 101-119.

402   The child was initially detained, was eligible for detention, or based on more recent information, would now be eligible for detention under Sections 201-206.

403   The Court has determined that placement of the child at disposition is **probable** and continued detention is required because the child may abscond or be removed from the jurisdiction of the court prior to disposition based upon consideration of the following factors:

     (a) the nature of the substantiated offense;

     (b) the child's employment and student status;

     (c) the nature of the child's family relationships;

     (d) the child's past and present residences;

     (e) the child's age, character, mental condition, previous juvenile record, and drug or alcohol addiction or substance abuse;

     (f) if the child has previously been released pending a court proceeding, whether the child appeared as required;

     (g) any other facts relevant to whether the child has strong ties with the community or is likely to flee the jurisdiction.

Note: The Juvenile Act, at 42 Pa. C.S. § 6341 (b), provides that upon entering a finding on the record that a child has committed the acts by reason of which he is alleged to be delinquent the Court "shall then proceed immediately, or at a postponed hearing, **which shall occur not later than 20 days after adjudication if the child is in detention,** to hear evidence as to whether the child is in need of treatment, supervision or rehabilitation and to make and file its findings thereon."

However, in cases where the disposition hearing is to be continued by the Court, the following shall apply:

A child whom the Court has found to have committed a delinquent act or to be a delinquent child may not be held in secure detention pending disposition for longer than 20 days from such adjudication or finding **absent an additional court appearance at which such period of detention is extended for good cause shown.** Any such detention shall be subject to review by the Court **at a hearing** every 10 days.

7/86

-24-

5. CIRCUMSTANCES UNDER WHICH SECURE DETENTION MAY BE ORDERED FOLLOWING DISPOSITION PENDING TRANSFER TO PLACEMENT:

Section

501   The child was found to be a delinquent child on the basis of an offense for which secure detention would be permitted pursuant to Sections 101-119.

502   The child was initially detained, was eligible for detention, or based on more recent information, would now be eligible for detention pursuant to Sections 201-206.

503   The child is awaiting placement in a Youth Development Center Secure Unit or other secure residential treatment program.

504   The child is awaiting placement and the Court has determined that secure detention is required pending transfer to such placement based upon consideration of the following factors:

    (a) the nature of the substantiated offense;

    (b) the child's employment and student status;

    (c) the nature of the child's family relationships;

    (d) the child's past and present residences;

    (e) the child's age, character, mental condition, previous juvenile record, and drug or alcohol addiction or substance abuse;

    (f) if the child has previously been released pending a court proceeding, whether the child appeared as required;

    (g) any other facts relevant to whether the child has strong ties to the community or is likely to flee the jurisdiction.

    Note: A delinquent child may not be held in secure detention under this section beyond 20 days from the date of the Order of Commitment or Placement in the absence of an additional court appearance extending such period of detention for good cause shown.

    Any further detention shall be subject to review by the Court every 10 days. (This review need not involve a court appearance.)

7/86

6. CIRCUMSTANCES UNDER WHICH SECURE DETENTION MAY BE AUTHORIZED ON THE BASIS OF THE CHILD'S STATUS PENDING OR SUBSEQUENT TO A DISPOSITION REVIEW PROCEEDING:

Section

601   A Disposition Review Proceeding is pending or has been held and the child is in placement in or is awaiting transfer to a Youth Development Center Secure Unit or other secure residential treatment program.

602   A Disposition Review Proceeding is pending or has been held and the child was returned from placement for failure to adjust.

603   A Disposition Review Proceeding is pending or has been held and secure detention is required based upon consideration of the following factors:

    (a) the nature of the substantiated offense;

    (b) the child's employment and student status;

    (c) the nature of the child's family relationships;

    (d) the child's past and present residences;

    (e) the child's age, character, mental condition, previous juvenile record, and drug or alcohol addiction or substance abuse;

    (f) if the child has previously been released pending a court proceeding, whether the child appeared as required;

    (g) any other facts relevant to whether the child has strong ties to the community or is likely to flee the jurisdiction.

7. CIRCUMSTANCES UNDER WHICH SECURE DETENTION MAY BE AUTHORIZED ON THE BASIS OF EXTRAORDINARY AND EXCEPTIONAL CIRCUMSTANCES.

Section

701   The child is not otherwise eligible for secure detention pursuant to the preceding standards; however, the facts present extraordinary and exceptional circumstances which require the use of secure detention. (The statement of reasons which accompanies any detention under this Section must include an explanation of why an exception was warranted and why non-secure options were rejected.)

    Note: Detention under this section may not be authorized routinely or because non-secure alternatives do not exist in adequate numbers, but only in the exceptional and extraordinary case.

    Secure detention is not to be used when a child **alleged** to be delinquent cannot be released **solely** because there is no parent, guardian or custodian **able** to assume responsibility or adequately supervise the child.

                                 7/86

Notes

1. Neither youth had any prior adjudications, and both had relatives present in court at the initial detention hearing. [Like many states, Pennsylvania requires that a detention hearing be held within seventy-two hours of a juvenile being placed in detention (42 Pa.C.S. §6332).] The Juvenile Court later dismissed the charges against one plaintiff, who had been detained for seventeen days prior to the adjudicatory hearing. The second plaintiff was adjudicated delinquent on charges of receiving stolen property and unauthorized use of auto. He remained in detention until his disposition hearing two weeks later, at which time he was placed on probation. He spent thirty-four days in detention.

2. The spirit of the settlement may endure beyond 1996. In the spring of 1991, Pennsylvania's multi-agency Juvenile Justice Task Force recommended that the *Coleman* standards continue as permanent criteria for admission to secure detention.

3. Annual detention admission rates will be higher, as a rule, than detention rates gleaned from point-in-time studies, in which analysis is made of the number of detainees on a particular day. Some juveniles may have been admitted several times during the year being analyzed.

Bibliography

Goldkamp, J. (1984). Characteristics of detention populations in selected Pennsylvania counties. Unpublished paper.

Legal Cases

Coleman v. Stanziani (no. 81–2215, E.D. Pa. 1981).
Pennsylvania Juvenile Act, 42 Pa.C.S. §6325.
42 Pa.C.S. §6332.
42 Pa.C.S. §6304.
570 F. Supp. 679 (E.D. Pa. 1983).
735 F. 2d 118 (3d Cir. 1984), *cert. denied* 469 U.S. 1037 (1984).
Schall v. Martin, 467 U.S. 253 (1984).
Coleman consent decree, April 18, 1986.

8

Implementing Detention
Policy Changes

WILLIAM H. BARTON

Human service policies are officially promulgated by legislative, judicial, or administrative bodies. Their implementation, however, rests in the many hands of agency staff at all levels who must adapt the policy to their working realities. It is no longer a surprise to learn that policies are rarely carried out exactly as intended or without unanticipated side effects. A growing body of literature has emerged to explain what happens between the formulation of a policy and the successful or unsuccessful achievement of its objectives.

Factors Affecting Policy Implementation

A number of analysts have suggested factors that can influence implementation (e.g., Van Meter & Van Horn, 1975; Berman, 1978, 1980; Bardach, 1977; Palumbo & Harder, 1981; Pressman & Wildavsky, 1973; Rice & Rogers, 1980; Sabatier & Mazmanian, 1981). While the emphases may vary, there is general agreement that the key factors include: the nature of the problem being addressed by the policy; the clarity of the policy; the commitment and capability of leadership; organizational relationships within and among implementing agencies; the balance of support and resistance in the political environment; and incentives and sanctions for compliance and noncompliance. Accordingly, the likelihood of successful implementation is enhanced when, among other things:

There are clear and consistent objectives.
There is an adequate causal theory: causal linkages are understood,

and officials responsible for implementation have jurisdiction over critical linkages.

Financial resources are adequate.

There is enabling legislation or clear policy mandates.

There is strong commitment from leadership.

The leadership skills of implementing officials are strong.

There is consensus among the relevant key actors—social conditions, public opinion, and key political figures support the policy.

There are adequate incentives for compliance and/or sanctions for noncompliance.

There is formal access by outsiders, e.g., oversight by supportive interest groups.

In sum, the implementation of policy change requires developing the political "will" to initiate the changes and the technical "way" to carry them out. The first three factors in the list above reflect technical requirements: goals (what to do), causal theory (how to do it), and resources (with what to do it). The rest of the factors reflect contextual variables affecting the political will to implement policies: mandates, leadership, consensus, incentives, and community support.

Some of these factors, such as the desirability of clear objectives and enabling legislation or mandates, are self-explanatory. Others merit further discussion here. An adequate causal theory means that there is a clear link between the actions prescribed by a policy and the objective it seeks to attain. Moreover, the key actions must be under the jurisdiction of implementing officials. Regarding juvenile detention, for example, the number and types of youths admitted to secure detention facilities are clearly linked to intake policies. A new intake policy promulgated by an executive branch agency would, by itself, have limited impact on a detention system in which the courts controlled intake decisions (although the link between intake procedures and detention usage is clear, the executive agency does not have jurisdiction over that critical linkage in this hypothetical example).

The importance of adequate financial resources should be obvious, but policies are often enacted without the provision of adequate resources. For example, the 1990 Florida juvenile justice reform legislation mandated a statewide system of case management for delinquency services, but only a portion of the funds needed to develop and implement that system were allocated. At best, the policy will be partially implemented, either in selected regions of the state or in selected parts of all districts.

The leadership factor cannot be overestimated. The implementation of a policy does not occur all at once, but rather evolves over a period of time. During that time, anticipated and unanticipated obstacles emerge and must be countered if the implementation is to remain on track. Feedback from early efforts may demonstrate that aspects of the policy need modification and refinement. Someone must shoulder the responsibility for managing the implementation process. Bardach (1977) coined the term "Fixer" to refer to a key actor in the implementation process who is highly committed to the goals of the policy and effectively able to intervene in the implementation process to counter opponents' moves and to keep proponents on track.

Although consensus among relevant key actors is highly desirable, it is rarely present initially. There are a variety of strategies for developing a consensus or for neutralizing opponents who cannot be otherwise persuaded to join a consensus. These will be discussed more below.

Any new policy or change in an existing policy requires various persons to change their usual way of doing business. Other things being equal, many people will resist such change. Incentives for compliance or sanctions for noncompliance—or both—can help encourage the changes. Such contingencies at an agency level can involve promotions, bonuses, etc., while at the broader level litigation, public relations campaigns, etc., can be effective. Litigation, in particular, will be discussed below, as it has played a major role in several detention initiatives.

Although human service agencies are responsible to the community, much of their day-to-day work goes unnoticed. Agencies develop informal relationships with each other and settle into routines that allow them to function smoothly while protecting their resources. As a result, the objectives of various policies, as they relate to the provision of service to the community, sometimes take a back seat to internal organizational goals. The more directly the community is involved in the implementation of a policy, the more likely it is that the agencies will be held accountable to the policy objectives in the implementation process. Ways to involve the community include the use of formal oversight committees and the inclusion of supportive community advocacy groups in policy planning and implementation monitoring.

Implementing Juvenile Detention Reforms

Technical Factors

For juvenile detention reforms, the technical "ways" are there—objective intake criteria, a range of alternative programs, diligent case monitoring, etc., as described in previous chapters. Given the presence of many relatively low-risk juveniles in secure detention, detention usage can be reduced by exerting stricter controls to limit intake, providing detention alternatives for the low-risk youths, and expediting the processing of detained youths to limit length of stay. Financial resources should be adequate, since non-secure detention alternatives generally cost less than secure detention.

Political Factors

Developing the political will to initiate changes and the leadership to implement and sustain them are more challenging. Rarely will the contextual variables all be favorable at the outset. Traditionally, juvenile justice has been marked by ideological schisms between "hard liners" who favor get-tough, punishment-oriented approaches and "reformers" who prefer to emphasize rehabilitative approaches. As can be inferred from the discussions in the first two chapters of this book, both sides have viewed detention as a catch-all resource and expanded its role far beyond its appropriate purpose. On the one hand, it is often used as summary punishment; on the other hand, in the absence of other adequate treatment resources, it is sometimes used as a way to provide some assessment and treatment services. Developing the political will to implement detention reforms of the kind advocated in this book requires that both sides adopt a narrower definition of detention and then decide how best to translate that definition into policies and procedures.

Strategies

Political will can be affected by consensus strategies, conflict strategies, or some combination of both. Consensus strategies focus on education, team building, and technical assistance. Conflict strategies include manipulations of political influence, bargaining, fiscal leverage, and sometimes threats of litigation. Both consensus and conflict strategies have been used in detention reform efforts, and both have their advantages and limitations. For example, consensus strategies may have a better potential for bringing about lasting change, but they generally take longer and are sometimes insufficient to overcome strong initial resistance. It is possible to use consensus and conflict strategies together in a reform effort, as was the case with the Broward detention project (see chapter 4).

Detention Reform Implementation Examples

Let us consider the four specific detention reform efforts discussed in this book—the Broward Detention Project (chapter 4); the Cuyahoga County experience (chapters 2 and 5); the Pennsylvania experience (chapter 7); and the San Francisco experience (chapter 3) —in terms of the implementation model discussed above. Table 8.1 displays the primary intervention strategies and an assessment of the implementation factors associated with each reform effort, to the extent that such information is presented in or can be inferred from the reports. While this comparative exercise is not a rigorous experiment, it may provide insights into the roles that various factors can play in such reform efforts.

Broward

The Broward Detention Project combined consensus and conflict strategies in its attempt to reduce the use of secure detention through the development of objective intake criteria, non-secure alternative detention programming, and diligent monitoring of detention usage. The pre-existing lawsuit against the detention center reflected an initial conflict strategy that proved to be necessary in order to get officials to assign high priority to detention and to attract the resources required to bring about the changes. The Project then turned to consensus strategies designed to bring the various key actors (court, prosecutors, public defenders, and service providers) together. These strategies included: education—information about model detention programs elsewhere, empirical feedback about Broward's detention usage, the link between intake procedures and detention usage, etc.; mediation to encourage settlement of the lawsuit; group facilitation through the use of a representative task force; and other liaison work (see the discussion in chapter 4 about the role of the project attorney-liaison).

The technical factors were favorable. The goals were clear—reduce the use of secure detention without compromising public safety. The causal theory was adequate in that it recognized the importance of intake screening, alternative programming, and careful monitoring. The resources were uncommonly adequate, given the support of the Annie E. Casey Foundation for managing the overall effort and starting up new alternative programming.

The political factors were mixed at the outset, but had improved considerably by the end of the project. The existing detention legislation at the beginning of the project presented several obstacles, particularly because it gave prosecutors the primary role in intake decisions.[1] In addition, the statutory detention intake guidelines were so broad that they permitted the secure detention of almost any youth. The juvenile justice reform legislation of 1990 included detention statutes that were highly supportive of the project's reform objectives: the prosecutors' role was greatly reduced, objective intake criteria were mandated, and non-secure alternatives were required statewide.

The commitment to detention reform among the leadership within the Department of Health and Rehabilitative Services (HRS), the agency responsible for operating detention, was mixed. Many at the state level were supportive, while some at the local district level were less so. The leadership at the state level frequently pressured the local district to implement detention reforms, but operational authority resided at the district level. The district administration dragged its feet on implementing some of the alternative programming, even though outside resources were provided. The district's legal counsel was also less than aggressive in monitoring and challenging inappropriate detention usage on the part of the court. During the course of the project and shortly after its completion, most of the district-level administrators had been replaced. The incoming officials were much more supportive of the reform objectives.

In a sense, the Center for the Study of Youth Policy, and Judge Frank Orlando in particular, assumed the role of "Fixer," negotiating with opponents and trying to keep HRS on track with procedures consistent with policy objectives. The Center for the Study of Youth Policy's temporary standing, lasting only for the two years of the Project, limited its appropriateness as a "Fixer." Judge Orlando, however, has continued in the role of "Fixer." He has served on state juvenile justice advisory boards, maintained close ties to legislators, and helped shape the reform legislation of 1990. He continues to assist the Broward HRS administration with detention issues.

There was no initial consensus among the key actors regarding the proper role of detention in the juvenile justice system. The court and prosecutors favored broad use of detention; HRS and the public defenders favored more limited use. There were few other voices heard. During the project period, the prosecutors became somewhat supportive, the court less so. However, subsequent turnover on the Juvenile Court bench has brought in judges who are much more supportive.

The incentives and sanctions provided by the lawsuit on the one hand, and the Casey Foundation on the other, were powerful forces and largely responsible for the initiation of the effort to change in spite of the other, less favorable political factors discussed above. The lawsuit has now been withdrawn and Casey Foundation funds are no longer provided, yet the reform policies have continued to flourish. Presumably, the positive results of the new policies have become somewhat self-sustaining, so that outside incentives and sanctions are less necessary.

Community involvement was minimal. A few attempts were made to involve advocacy groups, but they never developed a major role.

The initial results of the Broward project were moderately favorable. Secure detention use decreased substantially but still exceeded the facility's capacity. Alternatives were in place, if tentatively. Fortunately, with the statewide reform legislation and the subsequent changes in leadership and the judiciary, coupled with the continued involvement of Judge Orlando as a "Fixer," all helped further the gains. By the end of 1991, 19 months after the project had ended, secure detention use in Broward had plummeted to less than one-third of its capacity.

Cuyahoga County

The Cuyahoga County (Cleveland) scenario was somewhat different. Its detention center was operated by the court rather than a state agency, as had been the case in Florida. As Martin has demonstrated (see chapter 2), Cuyahoga County's use of secure detention has fluctuated widely over the last 20 years. For present purposes, we will focus on the period from 1985 to 1990. Faced with escalating secure detention rates and pressure to invest in costly additional beds, the key decision makers—chief judge, court administrator, and detention supervisor—chose to develop and implement policies designed to limit the use of secure detention.

The goal was clear: limit the use of secure detention. The causal theory was adequate: limit intake through the use of explicit screening criteria, establish alternative programs, and expedite cases through the system. Resources were adequate to develop the alternatives. Committed and competent leadership was responsible for the consensual development of a clear mandate. Given the consensus, additional incentives or sanctions were unnecessary at the beginning. Similarly, community involvement was neither necessary nor sought after to further the policy objectives. The Cuyahoga County scenario can best be described as self-contained within the boundaries of the court and heavily dependent upon the leadership. In this context, the successful implementation of policy changes was relatively easy to bring about, given the strength, commitment, and consensus among the leadership.

However, the very factors that facilitated the initial success of the Cuyahoga County effort made it vulnerable in the long run. In 1989, the leadership was replaced. The incoming key decision makers did not share the commitment to the reform goals and policies established by their predecessors. No incentives or sanctions existed to reinforce the reform policies, nor was there significant pressure from the outside community favoring the reforms. As a result, by 1990, the rate of secure detention in Cuyahoga County had surged upwards, reaching its earlier peak levels.

Pennsylvania

As described by Anderson and Schwartz (see chapter 7), a lawsuit filed in 1981 prompted detention reform in Pennsylvania. The parties reached a mediated settlement agreement in 1986 that included explicit intake standards for the use of secure detention. The agreement resulted in a substantial drop in the use of secure detention, although use has increased in more recent years, as will be further discussed below. Pennsylvania started with a conflict strategy (litigation), but moved toward consensus strategies (mediation, technical assistance) after both sides saw the necessity for a settlement. The Juvenile Court Judges' Commission (JCJC) played a key leadership role in defining, implementing, and monitoring the policy changes.

In terms of the technical implementation factors under consideration here, Pennsylvania had a reasonably clear goal: to reduce the use of secure detention. Pennsylvania's causal theory was limited to the link between intake criteria and secure detention usage, but did not extend to alternative programs for many typically detained youths nor aggressive expediting of cases in secure detention to minimize length of stay. There is no explicit mention of resources in the Anderson and Schwartz chapter, but we may assume that resources were adequate, since reducing secure detention use rarely costs more and usually costs less than the continued high rates of secure detention.

With one exception, the political factors appear to have been favorable by the time of the settlement agreement. Settlement of the lawsuit was an adequate incentive because it meant avoiding litigation costs and the costs associated with potential defeat, but also because it meant limiting the intrusion of the federal court into the state's authority to make and implement policy. JCJC was committed to resolving the lawsuit, recognized the value of consultation and mediation in the development of solutions, and was capable of influencing the courts throughout the state. The settlement agreement contained a clear mandate to implement more restrictive detention-intake guidelines. In retrospect, the only political factor lacking was community involvement.

Pennsylvania's experience is interesting in that, once JCJC assumed a leadership role, the reform process was fairly smooth and produced early favorable results with a minimum of controversy. As Anderson and Schwartz point out, the specific intake guidelines were sufficiently elastic to permit judges to retain considerable discretion. While this proved helpful in gaining compliance with the reform policies, it may have limited the long-term effectiveness of the reforms.

Specifically, the guidelines allowed detention of cases that did not otherwise meet the criteria if "the facts present extraordinary and exceptional circumstances which require the use of secure detention" or "the child presents extraordinary circumstances requiring secure detention to prevent him/her from absconding." The use of both discretionary categories has risen steadily, largely accounting for the recent increases in secure detention use. The lack of specificity regarding "extraordinary circumstances" permitted judges to regularly allow detention for certain offenses not specifically included in the guidelines, e.g., auto theft and drug law violations. Anderson and Schwartz rightly suggest that this elasticity prevented calls for a permanent modification to the guidelines addressing these specific offenses and thus resulted in less of an increase in detention usage than might have occurred otherwise.

Perhaps the Pennsylvania experience was less rancorous than some others because the interests of at least some of the usual opponents of detention reforms, such as judges, were well represented in the reform leadership. While JCJC is to be applauded for its enlightened leadership, one might still suggest that the long-term effectiveness of the policy changes will be modest. Other key factors that contribute to this mixed result are the limited causal theory employed and the lack of outside community involvement, as noted above.

San Francisco

In contrast to the Pennsylvania experience, the San Francisco experience, as described by Steinhart (see chapter 3), began with a consensus strategy but shifted to a conflict strategy that has certainly retained its adversarial character. Responding to the suicide of a youth in detention in 1986, San Francisco hired consultants to develop a new juvenile justice plan. In 1988, the National Council on Crime and Delinquency was enlisted to help implement some aspects of the plan. NCCD conducted research to estimate the number of detention beds required and proposed an objective risk screening tool to guide intake decisions. While supported by the leadership, the criteria met with strong resistance from some of the line staff. Overrides of the instrument were commonplace. Nevertheless, the risk screening helped bring about a modest reduction in the size of the detention center population.

Detention remains a volatile issue in San Francisco, with some politicians alleging that, contrary to available evidence, the new intake policies endanger public safety. On the other hand, uncommonly visible advocacy groups continue to push for reform. Conditions of confinement for those in detention have remained deplorable, however, resulting in the filing of a lawsuit in 1990 by public interest lawyers.

A consideration of the implementation factors provides some insights into the San Francisco experience. The goals and causal theory behind the reform effort were clear and adequate. Although the NCCD effort focused on intake criteria, a home detention alternative already existed, and the consultants kept advocating more creative responses to deal with uncooperative parents and other situations that often resulted in detention for youths who did not otherwise meet the intake criteria. No mention is made of the level of resources, but, as with the Pennsylvania example, we may assume that they were adequate, since reduced use of secure detention tends to produce savings.

The political factors were clearly mixed. There was little in the way of a formal mandate for the policy changes. Leadership changed during the intervention effort, and the new leaders were more committed to the reform objectives. There is not enough information in the report to determine the competence level of the leadership. One may speculate, however, that the escalating conflict could have been prevented had there been a truly effective "Fixer." Incentives were adequate: although San Francisco is faced with the likely necessity of constructing a new facility in any event, successful implementation of the reforms could limit the size, and thus the cost, of the new building. Moreover, the reforms could possibly have prevented the lawsuit, and could still contribute to a relatively speedy resolution of the litigation. As noted above, community involvement was higher and more influential than is usual in such scenarios. The main political shortcoming appears to have been the inability to develop and maintain a consensus concerning the reform objectives.

None of the above discussion is meant to imply that the reform effort was misguided or that it was unsuccessful. The discussion merely highlights the complexity of implementing policy change in as politically charged an area as juvenile justice. It is probably fair to say that the San Francisco effort is ongoing and that it may yet turn out to be highly successful. To this point, however, its effect has been modest.

Lessons Regarding Implementation of Detention Reforms

The analysis of the implementation scenarios of the four detention reform efforts provides some summary lessons for those seeking to implement such policy changes. Many of these lessons probably apply to other policy areas as well.

1. The problem of juvenile detention overuse is highly amenable to change. The technical implementation factors are relatively straightforward and likely to be favorable. In most jurisdictions, secure detention use *can* be reduced without jeopardizing public safety by (*a*) developing objective intake criteria, (*b*) utilizing alternative programming, and

(c) expediting the processing of detained youths to limit length of stay. These steps are not expensive and can usually be covered by savings from reductions in secure detention. Successful implementation is most likely when *all* of the technical factors have been addressed. For example, Pennsylvania's efforts might have been more successful had attention been paid to detention alternatives and case expediting in addition to intake criteria.

2. Among the political factors, leadership may be the most crucial. The eventual success of the Broward reforms and the initial success of the Cuyahoga County and Pennsylvania efforts were surely greatly facilitated by the presence of effective "Fixers." The subsequent turn-around in Cuyahoga County which accompanied the change in leadership only serves to underscore this point. Those initiating detention reform efforts should try to identify or develop someone or some group for the role of "Fixer."

3. The importance of developing a consensus should also be recognized. Although conflict strategies may be necessary to create sufficient initial motivation for change, reliance upon conflict strategies alone is unlikely to result in long-term adherence to reform policies. The problem with coercive strategies is that they can produce compliance only as long as the coercive threat is valid. Compliance produced by internalized change has a greater potential for long-term continuity. The fostering of internalized compliance may take a long time since it requires individualized educational strategies, technical assistance in staff development, and several iterations of pilot testing of new procedures.

Reform proponents should consider developing a stakeholders' group to participate in the design, monitoring, and evaluation of the policy implementation. This group must contain representatives from the major juvenile justice agencies and related interest groups in the community, i.e., the court, law enforcement, prosecutors, public defenders, youth corrections agency, child advocates, provider programs, etc. If possible, an outside facilitator with acknowledged expertise in juvenile justice issues as well as group techniques should lead the group. This group can be the target of early education efforts and can subsequently transmit this knowledge to others in the system.

In addition, consensus strategies should be extended to the line staff in agencies that will be directly affected by the reforms. Their input into certain implementation decisions may not only improve the procedures but also result in line staff "buying into" the reform objectives.

4. The incentive structure surrounding the implementation of a policy change warrants attention. One would think that the incentive structure inherent in detention reforms would be sufficient—more cost-effective handling of juveniles prior to their court hearings, more humane treatment of children, etc. However, detention has come to serve a number of interests in many juvenile justice systems; it is often made to compensate for the lack of sufficient child welfare services and other juvenile justice resources, such as commitment programs, etc. Changes introduced in detention practices may require adjustments in other parts of the child welfare and juvenile justice systems, and such adjustments may be resisted unless motivating mechanisms such as incentives and sanctions are included as part of the reform strategy. Such mechanisms can include outside grant support for the development of new programs, retraining of staff, monitoring and evaluation, etc. On the other hand, sometimes the incentive structure can be affected dramatically by the introduction of litigation, hence its frequent use in this area.

5. When possible, one should have the reform goals—and perhaps some of the technical procedures for achieving them—expressed as a formal mandate, through legislation if feasible. Such mandates provide additional authority to the leadership and can counter some of the resistance that might otherwise limit implementation success. The presence of mandates in Cuyahoga County in the form of formal court policy statements, in Pennsylvania through the JCJC, and, eventually, in Florida as part of the statewide reform legislation probably enhanced the success of those efforts. Of course, such mandates can change when those responsible for them change, as seen in Cuyahoga County.

6. Community involvement from advocates and others is perhaps most obviously helpful in situations which must rely on conflict strategies, as in the San Francisco example. It can also be useful in any situation to provide monitoring and continued influence to help maintain compliance with reform objectives over the long run.

Appendix: Table

Table 8.1
Implementation Scenarios for Four Detention Reform Efforts

	Reform Effort			
Implementation Factor	Broward	Cuyahoga	Pennsylvania	San Francisco
Primary strategy				
Consensus/conflict	both	consensus	both	conflict
Technical factors				
Clear goals	+	+	+	+
Adequate causal theory	+	+	o	+
Adequate resources	+	+	+	?
Political factors				
Legislation/mandate	−/+	+/−	+	o
Leadership commitment	o	+/−	+	o/+
Leadership competence	o/+	+	+	?
Consensus developed	−/o	+	+	−
Adequate incentives	+	o	+	+
Community involvement	o	o	o	+
Success of effort	o/+	+/−	o	o

Sources: For Broward, W. Barton et al., chapter 4; Cuyahoga County, Martin, chapter 2 and Sanniti, chapter 5; Pennsylvania, J. Anderson and R. Schwartz, chapter 7; San Francisco, Steinhart, chapter 3.

Key: 　+　factor generally favorable
　　　　−　factor generally unfavorable
　　　　o　factor relatively neutral
　　　　?　insufficient information in report
　　　　/　factor changed during course of intervention

Notes

Portions of this chapter have been adapted from William H. Barton, "Promoting Change in Juvenile Detention: The Broward County Experience," paper presented at the annual meetings of the American Society of Criminology, Baltimore, November 1990.

1. Prior to the 1990 reform legislation, the intake process for detention was as follows: a law enforcement officer would bring a youth to the detention center and request secure or home detention. A detention intake worker would review the case and make a separate recommendation. If the two disagreed, a prosecuting attorney would be called to resolve the dispute. Almost invariably, the prosecutors in Broward specify secure detention. Thus, detention intake staff had virtually no control over intake.

Bibliography

Bardach, E. (1977). *The implementation game.* Cambridge, MA: MIT Press.

Berman, P. (1978). The study of macro- and micro-implementation. *Public Policy, 26,* 157–84.

Berman, P. (1980). Thinking about programmed and adaptive implementation: Matching strategies to situation. In H. Ingram & D. Mann (Eds.), *Why policies succeed or fail.* Beverly Hills: Sage.

Palumbo, D., & Harder, M. (1981). *Implementing public policy.* Lexington, MA: Lexington.

Pressman, J., & Wildavsky, A. (1973). *Implementation.* Berkeley: University of California Press.

Rice, R., & Rogers, E. (1980). Reinvention and the innovation process. *Knowledge, 1,* 499–515.

Sabatier, P., & Mazmanian, D. (1981). The implementation of public policy: A framework of analysis. In D. Mazmanian and P. Sabatier (Eds.), *Effective policy implementation* (pp. 3–35). Lexington, MA: Lexington.

Van Meter, D., & Van Horn, C. (1975). The policy implementation process: A conceptual framework. *Administration and Society, 6,* 445–88.

9

Detention Reform from a Judge's Viewpoint

SHARON MCCULLY

Detention is a mainstay of the juvenile justice system, relied upon by judges as a site of safekeeping, a place where they can be sure a juvenile will not get into any more trouble and will not run away. Because of the security and reassurance offered by detention, judges are very defensive about preserving traditional detention as it has almost always been known in modern juvenile justice systems. Any suggested limitations or reforms of detention elicit howls of outrage and concern from most judges.

Juvenile Court judges are generally more proactive in community and social policy functions than other trial court judges. Indeed, Juvenile Court judges have always been urged by the Council of Juvenile and Family Court Judges and other organizations to be catalysts for change in their communities where children's issues are concerned. However, in the area of detention, it seems judges are usually most active in taking leadership roles to *resist* change. The focus of this chapter is to encourage judges to be active participants in detention reform, to help them recognize that detention may be seriously harmful and that it acts to curtail or deprive the liberty of more juveniles around the country than any other part of the juvenile justice system.

Liberty v. Custody

Judges need to first acknowledge there is an inherent evil in detaining a child in a secure facility such as most detention centers. That evil is, at its essence, the serious deprivation of personal liberty which is inherent in any order of detention. It is more than that, however. Young, early, or first offenders are often mixed with more seriously criminal offenders and are therefore exposed to the tutelage of more sophisticated juveniles. There is a significant loss of personal dignity involved in the mere booking of a child in most detention centers, with the loss of personal clothing, searches (often including strip searches), the wearing of institutional clothing, and the depersonalization that occurs within any correctional setting.

Although pretrial detention of juvenile offenders is routine in almost every state, and judges are given wide latitude by most statutes to impose pre-adjudication detention, judges should recognize that the decision to detain will have a profound effect on the life of a child and should be the exception rather than the rule in juvenile cases.

Since 1984, judges have taken solace from the United States Supreme Court decision in *Schall v. Martin*, 467 U.S. 253 (1984), in justifying traditional detention practices. In *Schall*, the Court upheld New York's statutory scheme of preventive detention, which actually provides more time limits and procedural safeguards than many other states' statutes but is otherwise reflective of traditional detention policies. The majority opinion in *Schall*, authored by Chief Justice Rehnquist, rationalizes the intrusion on liberty, which is acknowledged as substantial, with the theory that "juveniles, unlike adults, are always in some form of custody" (*Schall*, at 264). The Court seems to have little concern with significant differences between parental custody and secure detention, justifying detention as an appropriate *parens patriae* substitution for parental control.

In *In re Gault* in 1967, the Supreme Court discussed in detail the theory now espoused by the Court that juveniles have a right "not to liberty but to custody." It noted the theory, now embraced by Justice Rehnquist, that because a child has a right only to custody, "[i]f his parents default in effectively performing their custodial function— that is, if the child is 'delinquent'—the state may intervene. In doing so, it does not deprive the child of any rights, because he has none. It merely provides the 'custody' to which the child is entitled" (*Gault*, 387 U.S. 1, at 17). However, the Court rejected that theory emphatically, asserting that the *parens patriae* theory should not be used to rationalize exclusion of juveniles from the constitutional scheme. Although the present Court seems to have done an about-face on juveniles' rights in *Schall*, Juvenile Court judges should be urged to remember pre-Gault abuses of the juvenile justice system and refrain from taking the giant step backwards which might be suggested by the *Schall* decision.

Juvenile Court judges, who are believed to have a special concern for the best interests and welfare of children, should not ascribe to the theory that custody in secure detention is simply a substitute for parental custody when children are criminally misbehaving and that it is no more harmful than custody by parents. Surely any judge who has actually visited a detention center cannot compare the conditions of detention to those of a home under parental control. Even though almost all juvenile court statutes allow detention of a juvenile for his own protection, it cannot be said that confinement in a correctional institution such as a detention center is simply providing a safe place for a child to live while awaiting court action.

Though arguably endorsed by the *Schall* language, Juvenile Court judges should not accept the proposition that children have limited, if any, liberty rights. We should not regress from important strides made since *Gault* in recognizing and protecting the rights of juveniles in Juvenile Court proceedings. If anything, we should be *more*, not *less*, concerned about protecting juveniles' liberty interests, given the long-term serious harm that could result from even short-term stays in detention.

Is It Broke?

A typical response from judges when concerns about detention practices are addressed to them is that no one has demonstrated that there actually is a problem that needs fixing. The "if it ain't broke . . ." philosophy is strong among judges, who feel that there is nothing wrong with detention as it currently operates and that reformers are arguing for "change for change's sake" rather than for change needed to correct a harmful circumstance.

Institutional reform in juvenile corrections has usually come, if it has come at all, as a result of a crisis, often in the form of major civil rights actions. (Recall, for example, *Morales v. Turman*, in Texas; *Manning v. Matheson*, in Utah; and *In re Bobby M.*, in Florida.) Such a crisis response is certainly not the most desirable way to create change, but it will eventually become necessary if judges and juvenile justice officials do not take a proactive approach to detention reform before a crisis is created.

It probably isn't accurate to say that there is not a current crisis. One merely needs to look. Physical conditions of detention are often abominable. Detention centers have been neglected in favor of other institutional reforms necessitated by civil rights actions, riots, deaths, assaults, and other problems previously found in post-adjudication institutions, training schools, and the like. As a result, most physical facilities presently housing detention centers are outdated, overcrowded, and not amenable to humane, rehabilitative treatment models.

In addition, as resources continue to shrink for other services, many states seem to be increasing their use of detention. So more and more children are being exposed to the generally harmful effects of secure detention.

Further, only now are judges and others finding time to look at and seriously consider the constitutional parameters of detention practices. There are few, if any, restrictions on judicial discretion in detention decisions. Few states require even a probable cause finding prior to continuation of pre-trial detention. (In my district in Utah, probable cause hearings are held, but only as the result of a lawsuit which preceded the Supreme Court's decision in *Schall*. No other districts in Utah make formal probable cause determinations.) Counsel is most often not assigned until the adjudicatory phase, if at all, so the juvenile has no assistance of counsel when the detention determination is made. In most cases, no formal findings are required, even on the vague standards usually set forth for holding a child in detention, i.e., risk of further criminal acts, risk of non-appearance at future hearings, and protection of the juvenile. The judge need not set forth reasons for her finding that detention is justified on the basis of one of these factors, and the child has no opportunity to dispute or address the findings. Few time limitations are set by statute for pre-adjudication detention, although time standards are recommended by the ABA, and there were time limitations set forth in the New York statute at issue in *Schall*. What is presumably "short-term" pre-adjudication detention may turn into weeks or even months of secure confinement without benefit of almost any due process protections.

Therefore, even though there have been few major lawsuits creating sufficient crises in the detention area, Juvenile Court judges and other juvenile justice authorities should recognize that there is, indeed, a crisis in detention that needs our attention. We should be willing to act now, because it is the right thing to do, whether the Supreme Court, other courts, or state legislatures *require* us to do it or not. To borrow a phrase from Judge Orme of the Utah Court of Appeals, such a response is "an effort to move the standard of our performance from the floor toward the ceiling," or to go beyond "the permissible" to "the desirable." In other words, we should be willing to do what appears to be right, that which is to be desired, not just that which is required.

Standards for Detention

Most Juvenile Court statutes specify certain basic standards for detention of juveniles: (1) to compel appearance, (2) to protect the community by preventing further delinquent activity pending adjudication, and (3) to protect the juvenile. Using those standards as the foundation, judges should be encouraged, and should encourage their colleagues, to objectify those standards to the extent possible without unduly limiting necessary judicial discretion.

As is pointed out by the minority opinion in *Schall*, these basic standards, without further guidelines, can, and often do, result in unwarranted detention of many juveniles to their ultimate harm. There are no guidelines in most state statutes to assist a judge in determining on what basis he should decide when a juvenile is likely to miss future hearings, or commit further crimes in the foreseeable future, or seriously injure or hurt himself. Each of these standards bears more detailed consideration by judges and others in determining appropriate criteria for making detention decisions.

Failure to Appear

If a child is being held in detention to assure his appearance at future court hearings, there must be some objective basis for fearing he will not appear if sent home. Guidelines are quite easily formulated which would help measure the risk of failure to appear. For example, it should be verified that a child has a history of running away. It is also important that the "failure to appear" standard is not used as a way to hold simple runaways in detention in violation of federal rules prohibiting such practice. If the main reason a child is being held in detention is that he or she runs away from home, then the issue is certainly not one that should be handled by imposing the criminal-like approach of detention. Alternatives must be developed to treat and handle home runaways so that they do not end up in detention. The commission of a minor delinquent act, or even a status offense such as curfew violation or truancy, by a child with a history of running away from home should not qualify him to be held in detention. This would clearly be a "back door" approach to contravene the now generally accepted federal rules that runaways and status offenders should not be held in detention centers. A general rule should be that if the offense charged would not result in a detention order absent the history of running away from home, then the juvenile offender should not be held in detention simply because he is also a runaway.

A good guideline for avoiding failures to appear would be to determine whether the child has a history of missing court hearings after receiving legal notice—verifiable by a quick look at court records—or has a documented history of running away from court-ordered placements, i.e., probation, foster homes, correctional programs, etc. In other words, if the child has a history of following court-ordered restrictions, such as appearing at hearings, staying home while on probation, or maintaining in a community-based placement, there is little reason to doubt that he or she would appear in court after being ordered to do so.

There are certainly better alternatives possible to insure appearance than to hold a juvenile in secure confinement. Home detention, electronic monitoring, and restraints against parents are all good alternatives to detention for this purpose.

Objective guidelines are very appropriate for the failure-to-appear standard. It is one that is easily measurable by a juvenile's past history, either of missing hearings or of running from court-ordered placements. That history should be recent enough to be relevant to the current inquiry, i.e., within the last year. Such are the guidelines currently in use in my court as a result of a federal lawsuit and consent decree. This guideline is easily applied and rarely results in the release of a juvenile who subsequently fails to appear for an adjudication hearing.

Preventive Detention

It is preventive detention, or in other words, detention for the purpose of preventing further delinquent activity pending adjudication, which is the most problematic. Preventive detention of juveniles was specifically upheld as constitutional by the Supreme Court in *Schall*. The Court apparently was not impressed by expert testimony which negated the probability or accuracy of predicting future behavior, or by testimony of judges who actually applied the New York statute, both of which clearly indicated that preventive detention was, in fact, used by judges as a sanction for the current charge, to teach a lesson, etc. Although the Supreme Court indicated pre-adjudication detention would *not* be constitutional if it was, in fact, punishment, it seemed to ignore the reality that many of the judges did perceive and use pre-adjudication detention specifically as a sanction.

If prevention of future criminal activity is a justifiable reason to detain juveniles prior to a finding of guilt (and the Supreme Court says it is), then we must have some standards or guidelines to help us predict that risk. Surely it is not appropriate to detain *every* juvenile who commits a criminal offense to prevent him from further offending. But if every juvenile is not going to be detained for preventive purposes, how are we to determine which youths are going to be so detained?

Risk prediction instruments have been developed in many jurisdictions around the country. Some are quite extensive and detailed, others are fairly simple. All take into account the severity of the current offense, the history of other offenses and their severity, and the recency and frequency of such earlier offenses. Other factors such as substance abuse are also considered. Applying such instruments enables the judge to make a determination of future risk based on something more than "gut" feeling. While risk prediction instruments are certainly not guaranteed, they do reduce the likelihood of many youths being detained who present little or no risk of re-offending in the near future, and they increase the likelihood that those who present the more serious risks will actually be detained. The Broward County experience is a very good demonstration of the use of risk assessment instruments. Similar guidelines are in place in the Third District Court in Utah and a few other jurisdictions. It is important to note, anecdotally, that there was not a rash of crime committed by juveniles released under these guidelines. The experience is that most juveniles charged with a delinquent act can either be released under the supervision of their parents or guardians, or under other court-ordered restrictions, without jeopardizing community safety.

Offense-based guidelines seem to be an anathema to most judges, who believe factors other than the offense charged are more important in making detention decisions. However, if the concern really is pre-vention of further criminal behavior, what better measurement than current offense and offense history? If we cannot agree with that prem-ise, we are really going to have a difficult time arguing that what we are doing is preventive detention rather than punishment.

Another of the issues raised about preventive detention in the *Schall* case was that most of the juveniles held in pre-adjudication detention for purposes of preventing further criminal behavior were released after adjudication to non-secure placements, seemingly undermining the prevention argument. The Supreme Court found a legitimate state interest in preventing criminal activity, even for the short period dur-ing which a juvenile may be held (in New York) pending adjudication. The Court discounted clear evidence in the case that most juveniles went back to non-secure placements immediately following adjudica-tion, so that "prevention" was very short-lived. The dissent strongly disagreed with the majority position on this point.

The Supreme Court notwithstanding, it is important for judges to ask themselves what their real purpose is in detaining a youth pending adjudication. If the offense charged is one which is unlikely to result in secure confinement or very strict supervision after adjudication, most judges who honestly inquire of themselves would have to admit that prevention of future criminal activity is not a very sound basis for detention. Certainly victims of recidivist acts after adjudication are no less harmed than those who may be victimized by one awaiting adju-dication. Because it is doubtful that we, as a society, are willing to securely incarcerate, for the long term, every juvenile who commits a criminal offense of any kind, the incapacitation or prevention argu-ment is not a very persuasive one.

Again, alternatives to secure detention could be just as effective at preventing further criminal activity without the harmful effects of secure confinement. Courts which have tried closely supervised home detention, day treatment programs in lieu of detention, and electronic monitoring have had good success in maintaining juveniles in the com-munity without endangering public safety. (Examples are El Paso, Texas; most of Hawaii; Broward County, Florida; and several areas in Utah).

Judges must be willing to look at offense-based guidelines, with room for well-documented, clearly stated exceptions, to justify the use of pre-adjudication detention for preventive purposes. Otherwise, it can be much more persuasively argued that such detention is, in fact, pre-adjudication punishment.

Protection of the Juvenile

It is actually protection of the juvenile himself which is the argument most often set forth by opponents to limitations on detention. Judges often fall back on the traditional *parens patriae* doctrine, and the benevolent purposes of the Juvenile Court, to justify holding a child in secure detention for her own good.

Protective detention usually falls into three categories: (1) preventing a possibly suicidal child from harming himself; (2) protecting the juvenile from the folly of his or her own decisions which he or she has only limited capacity to understand (i.e., preventing further penetration into criminal activity or further activities which may be immoral, and emotionally or physically harmful, such as prostitution); and (3) protecting a child from an abusive or neglectful home environment.

As judges consider these protective reasons for detaining children in secure facilities, it should become painfully clear that detention centers are not appropriate places to accomplish these purposes. Surely a suicidal child cannot be helped, treated, or otherwise appropriately cared for in a detention center housing seriously criminal juveniles. Communities must develop alternatives to detention for this category of children for whom detention is clearly inappropriate. Crisis beds in hospitals are a necessity for a truly disturbed or suicidal child. Secure detention under conditions necessarily existing in most detention centers can only exacerbate the child's problems.

Protecting a child from his or her own folly is the most commonly cited reason for protective detention. The fundamental doctrine of the juvenile law is the incapacity of juveniles to fully comprehend the consequences of their acts. So, it is argued, juveniles who persist in committing acts which result in their involvement in correctional or court systems, and particularly which are harmful to their own physical and emotional well-being, must be detained for their own good. If one follows that argument, however, these juveniles would have to be detained for the duration of their minority; otherwise, the protective detention is, in fact, punishment. The good intentions and benevolence of judges who have a hard time releasing juveniles to further "mess up" their lives are not in doubt, but unless Juvenile Court judges are actually going to be deified, it is really not up to us to decide which juveniles we are going to detain in a correctional facility for their own good.

Further, if one applies commonly accepted mental health doctrines, the state is not constitutionally justified in curtailing liberty for protection of an individual against that individual's own desires. There is really no reason, not even the lack-of-capacity argument (which would apply equally to mentally ill adults), that such constitutional limitations should not also apply to juveniles who choose harmful lifestyles or activities. While all good Juvenile Court judges who are genuinely concerned about children are tempted to use our better judgment to protect juveniles from their own detrimental behavior, we must confine ourselves to constitutional uses of our authority.

Protective detention seems to be utilized more often for girls than for boys in the juvenile system, reflecting the paternalistic traditions of juvenile justice. Most juvenile court judges, including women, are unwilling to let girls be used, abused, and subjected to numerous indignities on the streets. While I share those concerns, and I personally abhor ingrained attitudes and traditional roles of our society which subject women in general to such atrocities, I cannot justify subjecting girls to yet another loss of personal control and liberty by placing them in secure correctional facilities to protect them from their own choices. Again, alternatives must be developed to assist courts in releasing such girls to placements outside secure correctional settings. We are stretching the bounds of constitutional acceptance by using detention as a holding facility for promiscuous, prostituting, street-walking juvenile girls.

The third category of protective detention is detention of youths who come from abusive or neglectful homes. Indeed, some youths prefer life in a detention center to life in their own homes. However, such children are clearly more appropriate for the child welfare system than for the delinquency/detention system. Detention should never be used for children who are within the jurisdiction of the Juvenile Court solely because they are victims of abusive or neglectful parents. To subject them to the harmful effects of detention, not just physically but also emotionally, is to further abuse them.

Guidelines

Relatively objective guidelines are recommended for both of the first two general purposes of pre-adjudication detention, to compel appearance and to prevent further criminal activity. (The third purpose, protection of the child, is an inappropriate use of detention altogether, and alternatives should be utilized.)

Judges nearly always have strong, negative reactions to the mere suggestion of guidelines, either for sentencing or detention. The only reason for such reaction seems to be the perception that guidelines severely limit judicial discretion. ("What do we need judges for if a computer can make these decisions?") Judicial authority and discretion are sacred cows, and there is no question that qualified, well-trained judges can be trusted to exercise discretion in a responsible manner.

It is baffling, however, that judges so strenuously resist the idea of tools that can help them exercise their discretion in more rational, explainable ways. As a judge who has used guidelines in one form or another from the beginning of my judicial experience, I can attest that the guidelines soon become ingrained as measures easily applied in individual cases, so that the judge soon forgets the guidelines themselves because the criteria seem so reasonable. Guidelines need not be severe restrictions on judicial authority; rather, they give the judges bases for making decisions they might otherwise want to make but cannot justify under more traditional, broad detention standards. For example, judges are often faced with parents who do not want to take their child home and then bring him or her back to court for an adjudicatory hearing. They want their child to stay in detention and learn a lesson. Often, the parents outright refuse to take a child home. Guidelines, either statutory or voluntary, give the judge a firm basis for insisting that parents take responsibility for their own children, relieving the court and overcrowded detention facilities from having to do the parents' job.

Guidelines limiting use of detention also tend to force development of alternatives. It was not until admissions guidelines limited use of pre-adjudication detention in my jurisdiction that alternatives such as home detention, crisis hospital beds, a group holding facility for child-welfare children (chins, pins, status offenders, and neglect and dependency victims), and diversion programs were developed. All are now currently in place because we simply refuse to admit those children to detention under our guidelines. Almost all judges would prefer to use non-secure, less intrusive alternatives to detention for many youths who are otherwise confined if such alternatives were available. Implementation of admissions guidelines can be of great assistance in forcing development of such alternatives.

Post-Adjudication Detention

Use of detention as a sanction, either for contempt of court or as a legislatively allowed dispositional alternative, is increasing, and it is now one of the most common causes of juvenile detention. For example, although admissions guidelines in my jurisdiction resulted in significant population reductions in the detention center five years ago, use of detention as a penalty for contempt of court, along with use of short-term detention as a disposition, which was authorized by legislation in 1988, have resulted in at- or over-capacity populations in our detention center on a daily basis.

Use of detention as a post-adjudication sanction cannot simply be dismissed by reformers as inappropriate and receive no more attention than that. Enforcement of court orders through imposition of detention time for contempt is a traditional use of detention and is seen as an inherent power of the court. It is really the ultimate use of judicial authority, and it cannot lightly be restricted or removed. Even federal restrictions on detention of status or other non-criminal offenders allow the use of detention to enforce "valid court orders." The "valid court order" exception is commonly used, either explicitly or through contempt proceedings.

Further, my experience has been that with the advent of short-term detention as a dispositional alternative, the use of suspended or stayed detention orders can effectively circumvent admissions guidelines. A juvenile who is arrested for an offense which would not qualify for admission to detention may be admitted if he has a stayed or suspended order of detention as a disposition. It has become fairly routine to issue such orders in my court, and so admissions guidelines have become almost a nullity, except for first-time offenders who are not under the continuing jurisdiction of the court in any capacity.

It is easy for those who have never sat behind a bench to say judges should not impose detention for contempt. However, when a youth repeatedly ignores, defies, and refuses to obey reasonable orders of the court, it is not so easy to restrain oneself from punishing such defiance by ordering detention. This is especially true because there are simply no available alternatives to detention as a sanction for contempt. Ordering additional fines to a juvenile who fails to pay fines and restitution is laughable, at least to the juvenile. Ordering house arrest to a probationer who is regularly violating all the other rules of probation simply gives him one more rule to ignore. So, judges routinely order time in detention.

It is an important challenge for those who seek to reduce detention populations, and who particularly disagree with the use of detention as a sanction, to develop creative alternatives which would be available to judges as sanctions, either for contempt or for delinquent acts. Until such alternatives are available, the use of detention as a sanction will continue to increase, perhaps becoming the category of greatest use of detention by judges.

In addition to the need for corrections systems to develop alternatives to detention as a sanction, judges should use as much restraint as possible in utilizing this option. When looked at realistically, ordering a youth to spend time in detention rarely accomplishes much in terms of greater compliance with court orders; it seldom results in more prompt payment of financial obligations, more strict compliance with terms of probation, less substance abuse, or more respectful behavior in the court room. What it does accomplish is satisfaction of the court's need to exact vengeance, which has little place in juvenile justice.

Community Involvement

If detention reform is to be successful, the onus should not rest primarily on the shoulders of judges, who often bear all of the political consequences for limitations or restrictions on "get tough" use of detention. With juvenile crime, and especially gang activity, on the rise in many areas, and communities and neighborhoods up in arms about uncontrolled juvenile delinquency, courts will be hard-pressed to justify limiting the use of detention. Therefore, reformers, including judges, need to involve other parts of the community in detention reform efforts. Police departments need to participate in setting guidelines and policies. Drop-off facilities need to be developed to allow police to take a non-detainable child to a designated point where someone else will take the burden of locating a responsible adult to whom the child can be released, so police officers can do their jobs on the streets. Legislators need to be educated on the harms inherent in secure detention of juveniles and encouraged to fund alternatives and set policies against the wholesale use of detention. Public hearings and media briefings should be held so that judges don't have to be seen as having sole responsibility for detention reform. Limitations on the use of detention will be less popular with the general public than with those who are educated and knowledgeable about juvenile justice. The symbol of juvenile justice is the judge, and, for good or bad, judges are credited with whatever the public sees happening in their community. Efforts should be made to minimize the political risks to judges from detention reform.

Conclusion

Detention has long been an integral part of the Juvenile Court and youth corrections systems. As stated elsewhere in this book, the inherent harms of secure detention, even on a short-term basis, are seldom recognized. Thus, there have been few reform efforts directed at detention. As a result, judges generally do not feel that the detention system is in need of reform or limitation. However, as judges are asked to evaluate honestly their traditional uses of detention, many will realize that many juveniles are being inappropriately detained and that even short-term detention carries with it the potential for serious harm, as well as for violations of liberty rights.

Judges should take a proactive role in limiting their own uses of detention and in encouraging the development of alternatives to traditional secure detention. Juvenile Court judges should be willing to participate in these reforms, even though not required by the Supreme Court, because it is the "right" thing to do, and because it will result in better, more humane, and more constitutional treatment of juvenile offenders in most communities.

Legal Cases

Schall v. Martin, 467 U.S. 253 (1984).
Schall at 264.
In re Gault, 387 U.S. 1 (1967), at 17.
Morales v. Turman, in Texas.
Manning v. Matheson, in Utah.
In re Bobby M., in Florida.

What Policymakers Need to Know about Juvenile Detention Reform

IRA M. SCHWARTZ

Juvenile detention is the underbelly of the juvenile justice system. Detention centers are isolated from the community and unmonitored by the media and most child advocates. About the only time the public hears about their local detention center is when a scandal—e.g., suicide, staff abusing youth, or an escape—surfaces in the press or on television.

While these institutions are hidden from public scrutiny, they are a grim reality to the hundreds of thousands of young people confined in them each year. Most of the juveniles locked up in detention centers on any given day are confined in antiquated, overcrowded, inadequately staffed, and poorly managed facilities. When pressed to act, policymakers and juvenile justice officials generally respond to the overcrowding and deteriorating physical plants by proposing to build new facilities or increasing the capacities of existing institutions. This occurs despite increased competition for shrinking public resources and evidence that large numbers of admissions can be prevented without compromising public safety.

What Accounts for the Over-Reliance on Detention?

The contents of this book make one thing clear: admissions to secure detention are primarily the result of policy decisions. More often than not, they are policies that have little to do with juvenile crime prevention or control. For example, Terry Martin's chapter describing the detention facility planning process in Cuyahoga County (Cleveland), Ohio is a case in point. Martin documented the fact that fluctuations in admissions to secure detention were largely related to juvenile court policies. Admissions were driven by judicial attitudes regarding who should be confined and not by rates of serious juvenile violent offenses and property crimes. As a result, there were years when many juveniles were admitted to secure detention who clearly could have been managed in less restrictive alternatives.

The chapter by Barton, Schwartz, and Orlando describing the developments in Broward County (Ft. Lauderdale), Florida is another example. In Broward County, dangerous overcrowding and unconstitutional conditions of confinement were effectively addressed by developing objective detention intake criteria, increasing the use of release on recognizance, and establishing a few carefully planned, community-based alternatives. The detention intake criteria, which were developed by judges, prosecutors, public defenders, law enforcement officials, and child advocates, limited the use of secure detention to youth accused of serious violent crimes who therefore presented a clear and substantial threat to the community. The current average daily population in the Broward County detention center is less than 60. Four years ago, the average daily population was in excess of 175.

Staff from the Conservation Company and the Juvenile Law Center in Philadelphia studied the fiscal implications of the reforms in Broward County. The preliminary findings indicate that Broward County officials "significantly reduced . . . long-term operating costs without jeopardizing public safety" (The Conservation Company and Juvenile Law Center, 1992, 1). This is something that should be of particular interest to elected public officials and juvenile justice professionals in other jurisdictions interested in controlling juvenile justice system costs.

David Steinhart describes the developments leading to the decline in admissions to San Francisco's detention facility. As in the case of Broward County, the decline resulted from changes in policies and practices. The policy changes were triggered by scandals that surfaced in the media, pressure for reforms by a community advocacy group, studies indicating that admissions could be reduced without compromising public safety, and because of the appointment of a new chief probation officer committed to controlling detention utilization. To a significant extent, and in the face of stiff opposition from unionized staff, admissions were gradually brought under control through the development, implementation, and monitoring of detention-intake screening criteria.

There are some who believe that simply creating alternatives to secure detention will curb admissions. It is not uncommon, for instance, for judges to say that they would reduce their reliance on detention if they had other alternatives. While this is a perfectly reasonable position, it rarely happens in the real world. There are many jurisdictions where alternatives were created. In virtually all instances, such alternatives had little or no sustained impact on reducing rates of admission to secure detention. In order to have the desired impact, community-based alternatives must be accompanied by the political will and commitment on the part of key policymakers and juvenile justice actors to control detention utilization.

The politicization of the juvenile crime problem is another major factor that contributes to the excessive use of detention. Put simply, judges who want to give the appearance of being "tough" on juvenile law violators will lock up lots of kids. Prosecutors claiming to protect the public by "cracking down" on juvenile crime often advocate for increased and virtually indiscriminate use of detention. This is particularly the case in jurisdictions where judges and prosecutors are elected and where they may have hopes of running for some other political office (i.e., governor, U.S. Senate, U.S. House of Representatives, state Supreme Court, etc.).

The politicization of juvenile crime may be good politics and may even help win elections. It also leads to bad public policy and is costly to the public. It also drains resources desperately needed for such other vital services as education, prenatal care, child welfare, health and mental health care, and services to the elderly.

The decade of the 1990s is shaping up as one of the most challenging in our national history. States and counties will continue to be faced with budget deficits and fiscal problems. Government officials will be forced to make difficult decisions and, in all likelihood, reduce the amount of public services. While this will prove to be a painful experience, it does provide some opportunities. For those who are willing and who have the courage to take on the challenge, it will provide an opportunity to reform detention systems.

Agenda for Reform

Policymakers and juvenile justice professionals seriously interested in reforming their youth detention systems should consider the following:

1. Conducting a comprehensive study of the detention system. The study should carefully and objectively examine detention intake criteria, admissions trends and reasons for admission to detention, length of stay in secure care, and the processing and handling of youth throughout the entire detention system. The study should also examine existing alternatives to detention and determine how well they are functioning. If at all possible, and for obvious reasons, the study should not be conducted by an architect or an architectural-planning firm.

Where such studies have been done, they have always identified large numbers of youth who could be diverted from secure detention. They also help to identify policies and practices that could be modified that would have a significant impact on controlling detention utilization.

2. Adopting objective detention intake criteria. The detention intake criteria recommended by the Institute for Judicial Administration/ American Bar Association and the National Advisory Committee on Juvenile Justice should be used as reference material in this process.

3. Developing 24-hour face-to-face detention intake screening and crisis intervention services. In jurisdictions with small numbers of referrals, detention screening and crisis intervention services should be available on an on-call basis. The purpose of face-to-face detention screening should be to carefully assess each referral and to insure that only those who meet criteria are admitted. The screening should also be designed to insure that appropriate decisions are made about returning youths to their homes and referring them to various alternative services.

4. Eliminating the practice of committing youth to serve time in detention. Youth who fail to obey probation orders or who engage in other non-dangerous and non-violent behavior need not be held accountable by having them committed to detention at an average cost of about $100 a day. Instead, they could be put under very intensive and virtually 24-hour supervision and ordered to pay restitution, perform work for their victims, or do community service. Although intensive supervision and surveillance is expensive, it is not nearly as costly as committing youth to detention. In addition, having youth make resti-

tution to their victims and perform community service is much more productive than simply incarcerating them.

5. Creating a detention population management position, particularly in large jurisdictions. The person who occupies this position should be responsible for monitoring detention intake decisions to make sure that only youth who meet criteria are admitted, monitoring cases admitted to detention and cases referred to alternatives to make sure they are processed expeditiously, and monitoring conditions under which youth are confined. Inappropriate admissions, cases lingering in detention status, unconstitutional conditions of confinement, and unprofessional practices should be brought to the attention of judges, detention administrators, defense attorneys, and other appropriate officials for corrective action. If necessary, they should be brought to the attention of the media.

6. Developing partnerships between public and private agencies in the delivery of alternative services. This will help to strengthen and build community support for alternatives and take advantage of existing community resources. The day report center operated by the Boys and Girls Clubs of Broward County (Ft. Lauderdale), Florida is a case in point. Boys and Girls Clubs' facilities are not generally used during the day. Contracting with them to provide an alternative to secure detention takes advantage of their facilities, helps to acquaint hard-to-reach youth with Boys and Girls Club programs, and builds support for community-based services.

7. Enacting legislation that restricts the use of detention and provides fiscal incentives to reduce admissions. One of the most effective strategies for reducing detention would be to enact legislation that included strict criteria for the use of secure detention. Such a strategy would be particularly effective if it also included funds that were distributed to localities as incentives for reducing rates of detention admissions.

8. Creating a range of alternatives to secure detention and criteria for their use. In addition to crisis intervention services, the alternatives should include such things as release on recognizance, home detention, family shelter care, staff-operated shelter care, and day report centers.

9. Developing a mechanism for overseeing and monitoring the detention system. Unless monitored on an ongoing basis, the problems that once plagued a detention facility tend to reappear.

Conclusion

The chapters in this book are authored by some of the most knowledgeable professionals in the country on the subject of juvenile detention. The chapters are brimming with useful information for policymakers and practitioners. Taken collectively, the chapters present clear and convincing evidence that detention need not be a degrading and dehumanizing experience and that it can perform the role for which it was intended: to house juveniles who present a clear and substantial threat to the community and who are at great risk to abscond pending their appearance in court.

Unfortunately, there is one thing this book cannot do. It cannot reform state and local detention systems. It is hoped, however, that it will both serve as a catalyst and provide support for those who might be willing to lead the fight.

Bibliography

The Conservation Company and Juvenile Law Center. (1992, November). *Preliminary cost analysis of the Broward County juvenile detention system transition 1987–1992*. Unpublished manuscript. Philadelphia, PA.

Contributors

James E. Anderson has been the executive director of the Pennsylvania Juvenile Court Judges' Commission since 1986. He was the principal drafter of the "Standards Governing the Use of Secure Detention," which were adopted by the commission as the basis for settlement in the Coleman detention case in Federal Court in 1986. Mr. Anderson is a frequent lecturer and trainer on topics related to juvenile justice and legislative advocacy.

William H. Barton is an associate professor in the School of Social Work at Indiana University, Indianapolis. From 1988 to 1992 he was a senior research associate with the Center for the Study of Youth Policy at the University of Michigan, where he was involved in the Broward County Detention Project described in this book. His current focus is on program evaluation and policy research in human services, especially in the areas of juvenile justice, child welfare, and domestic violence.

Joseph T. Christy is director of the Washington County, Oregon, Juvenile Department. From 1980 to 1991 he was director of the Shuman Juvenile Detention Center in Allegheny County, Pittsburgh, Pennsylvania. Since 1989 he has been editor of the *Journal for Juvenile and Detention Services*, a publication of the National Juvenile Detention Association.

Teri K. Martin is the proprietor of Law & Policy Associates, based in Oregon, a consulting enterprise specializing in juvenile and criminal justice system planning, research, and policy analysis. She has collaborated with juvenile justice policy makers in a variety of jurisdictions to develop improved decision-making policies and to evaluate the impact of policy and program changes on system effectiveness.

Judge Sharon P. McCully has served on the Third District Juvenile Court in Salt Lake City, Utah, since July 1983. Before her appointment to the bench, she was an assistant Utah attorney general. She is an active member of the National Association of Women Judges, the Judicial Council of the National Center for the Study of Youth Policy, the National Council of Juvenile and Family Court Judges, and the Utah Board of Juvenile Court Judges.

Judge Franklin A. Orlando (Ret.) is the director of the Center for the Study of Youth Policy at Nova Southeastern University, Shepard Broad Law Center, in Fort Lauderdale, Florida. For twenty-one years he was general counsel and executive director of the Joint Legislative Committee on Juvenile Justice and circuit judge in the state of Florida. He has twice been awarded the Florida Council on Crime and Delinquency Distinguished Service Award, and in 1993 he was the recipient of the American Bar Association Livingston Hall Juvenile Justice Award.

Carl V. Sanniti currently serves as the Cleveland regional administrator for the Ohio Department of Youth Services. He has previously served as the delinquency program administrator for the State of Florida District Team and the manager of alternative detention for the Cuyahoga County Juvenile Detention Center. He is the author of numerous articles on detention overcrowding and on methods to improve the use of juvenile detention in America.

Ira M. Schwartz is dean of the School of Social Work and director of the Center for the Study of Youth Policy (CSYP), University of Pennsylvania. From 1987 until 1993 he was professor and director of the CSYP at the University of Michigan's School of Social Work. Professor Schwartz served as the administrator of the Office of Juvenile Justice and Delinquency Prevention, U.S. Department of Justice, between 1979 and 1981. Previously, he directed criminal and juvenile justice agencies in the states of Illinois and Washington and worked extensively in both the public and private sectors. He is the author of numerous articles on juvenile justice and of *(In)Justice for Juveniles: Rethinking the Best Interest of the Child*, and *Juvenile Justice and Public Policy: Toward a National Agenda*.

Since 1982 **Robert G. Schwartz** has served as the executive director of the Juvenile Law Center, which he cofounded in 1975. He is a member of Pennsylvania's Juvenile Justice Task Force and chair of the American Bar Association's Juvenile Justice Committee. He has written extensively on service coordination and placement prevention in the child welfare and juvenile justice systems, testified before congressional and Pennsylvania legislative committees, and represented children in state and federal class action litigation, as well as in abuse, neglect, and delinquency cases in juvenile and family court.

David Steinhart is a Marin County, California, attorney and juvenile justice specialist. He is the author of numerous publications on public policies affecting children and youth, and was the principal draftsman of California legislation removing children from adult jails. From 1988 to 1992 he served as director of policy development for the National Council on Crime and Delinquency. In that capacity, he directed projects establishing juvenile criteria in three large California counties.

Deborah A. Willis is a doctoral student in the Social Work and Social Sciences Department at the University of Michigan.

Index

Alleghany County (Pittsburgh, Pa.) detention center. *See* Shuman Center
American Bar Association, 20, 179
American Correctional Association, 20, 117, 121, 126
Annie E. Casey Foundation, 69, 70, 76
Austin, J., 68

Baird, S. C., 81, 96
Ball, R. A., 6, 10
Bardach, E., 147, 149, 161
Barton, W. H., 3, 5, 11, 20, 28, 68, 69, 76, 96
Battle, J., 13, 28
Berman, P., 147, 161
Bishop, D., 4, 10
Broward County Detention Project (Fort Lauderdale, Fla.), 5, 6, 69–96, 104–5, 151–53, 177
  admissions, 84–86, 90–91, 92–94, 136
  alternatives to detention, 73, 76, 77–79
  and local Boys Club, 78–79
  and Community Youth Leaders, 78
  detention task force, 81, 83
  goals of, 69, 76–77
  and historical trends in the county, 90–94
  implementation of, 76–83
  intake screening, 79–81, 104, 177
  and Lutheran Ministries of Florida, 79
  overcrowding, 87
  pre-project crisis, 71–76
  public defender's involvement in, 81–82
  results of, 158
    changes in detention usage, 84–89, 151–53
    continued overcrowding, 87

    in costs, 86–87
    risk assessment instrument, 79–81, 82, 83, 104
    See also Florida
Broward Regional Juvenile Detention Center, 69, 107
  goals of, 104–5, 177
  See also Broward County Detention Project
Butts, J. A., 76, 96

California, 47–68, 156–57, 177
  average daily populations, 59
  detention problems, history of, 53, 56
  juvenile arrest rates, 48, 53
  overcrowding, 47–48, 59
  public safety issues, 60–63
  San Francisco, 53–64
  screening criteria, 48–64, 156, 178
    and effects on population levels, 59–60
    and management issues, 56–57
    monitoring of, 63–64
    and override practices, 58–59
    and release performance results, 62–63
  Youth Guidance Center, 53–55, 59–60, 61–62
Center for the Study of Social Policy, 8, 10, 13, 86, 96
Center for the Study of Youth Policy, 5, 69, 70, 76, 104, 152
Chesney-Lind, M., 17, 28
child advocacy organizations, 53
Children in Custody biennial census, 13, 28, 47
  limitations of data of, 14
child welfare issues, 159, 170, 171, 172
coalition building, 116–17

187